C-1681 CAREER EXAMINATION SERIES

This is your PASSBOOK for...

Supervisor of Accounts

Test Preparation Study Guide
Questions & Answers

NATIONAL LEARNING CORPORATION®

National Learning Corporation

212 Michael Drive, Syosset, NY 11791
(516) 921-8888 • www.passbooks.com
E-mail: info@passbooks.com

PASSBOOK® SERIES

THE *PASSBOOK® SERIES* has been created to prepare applicants and candidates for the ultimate academic battlefield – the examination room.

At some time in our lives, each and every one of us may be required to take an examination – for validation, matriculation, admission, qualification, registration, certification, or licensure.

Based on the assumption that every applicant or candidate has met the basic formal educational standards, has taken the required number of courses, and read the necessary texts, the *PASSBOOK® SERIES* furnishes the one special preparation which may assure passing with confidence, instead of failing with insecurity. Examination questions – together with answers – are furnished as the basic vehicle for study so that the mysteries of the examination and its compounding difficulties may be eliminated or diminished by a sure method.

This book is meant to help you pass your examination provided that you qualify and are serious in your objective.

The entire field is reviewed through the huge store of content information which is succinctly presented through a provocative and challenging approach – the question-and-answer method.

A climate of success is established by furnishing the correct answers at the end of each test.

You soon learn to recognize types of questions, forms of questions, and patterns of questioning. You may even begin to anticipate expected outcomes.

You perceive that many questions are repeated or adapted so that you can gain acute insights, which may enable you to score many sure points.

You learn how to confront new questions, or types of questions, and to attack them confidently and work out the correct answers.

You note objectives and emphases, and recognize pitfalls and dangers, so that you may make positive educational adjustments.

Moreover, you are kept fully informed in relation to new concepts, methods, practices, and directions in the field.

You discover that you are actually taking the examination all the time: you are preparing for the examination by "taking" an examination, not by reading extraneous and/or supererogatory textbooks.

In short, this PASSBOOK®, used directedly, should be an important factor in helping you to pass your test.

SUPERVISOR OF ACCOUNTS

DUTIES

Under general supervision, an incumbent of this class is responsible for supervising and coordinating the activities of an assigned unit of the accounts division. An incumbent supervises staff involved in the billing and collection of bills from third party reimbursement agents, private insurance carriers or as direct payment for services received. Supervision is exercised over a number of billing and collection clerks. Does related work as required.

SUBJECT OF EXAMINATION

The written test is designed to test for knowledge, skills, and/or abilities in such areas as:

1. Arithmetic computation;
2. Clerical operations with letters and numbers;
3. Name and number checking;
4. Office record keeping; and
5. Supervision.

Table of Contents

This test guide covers the majority of the subject areas for the examinations held in the Higher Level Account Clerical examination series. Most candidates will only be taking a small number of examinations involving only some of the subject areas. Candidates should focus their attention on those subject areas they will actually be taking. See page 3 of this test guide for more information.

GENERAL INFORMATION

Introduction: The information presented below may help you in preparing to take one or more of the examinations in this examination series.

Determining the Subject Areas in your examination(s): To determine the subject areas that are included in your examination(s), you should refer to the Examination Announcement(s) for the particular examination(s) you will be taking. The subject areas are listed under the heading "Subjects of Examination." Most candidates will be taking a small number of examinations covering only some of the subject areas included in this guide. It is recommended that you focus your preparation on the subject areas that are in the examination(s) you will be taking. Please Note: While this test guide provides information on many of the subject areas in the Higher Level Account Clerical examination series, it may not provide information for all the subject areas in your examination.

If you are taking more than one examination in this examination series and you compare the Examination Announcements for them, you may see that some subject areas are included in more than one of your examinations. Generally, there will be only one set of questions used for each subject area. So, for example, if you are taking three examinations, and all three include the subject areas "Office Record Keeping" and "Arithmetic Computation with Calculator," you will have to answer the questions in these subject areas only once in order to get credit for them on all three examinations.

Using the Candidate Directions provided at the test site: When you take your examination(s), you will be given a set of Candidate Directions. Read these very carefully so that you correctly identify the blocks of questions you need to answer for the examinations you are taking. Any block of questions that is part of more than one of your examinations only needs to be answered once. You will get credit for those questions on all of your examinations in which they appear.

Test questions: All the test questions included in the Higher Level Account Clerical examination series are multiple-choice questions. See the s*ample questions* in the subject area sections in this test guide for examples.

GENERAL INFORMATION – CONTINUED

Subject area information: After the list of subject areas, information is provided on how candidates will be tested in each of the subject areas listed. For each subject area, a Test Task is provided. This is an explanation of how questions will be presented and how to correctly answer them. Read each explanation carefully. (Please note: This test guide may not provide information on every subject area included in your examination.)

Sample questions: This test guide provides at least one sample question for each subject area listed. The sample questions will be similar to what will be presented in the test booklet(s). This test guide provides the Solution and correct answer for each sample question presented. You should study these in order to understand how the correct or best answers were determined.

LIST OF SUBJECT AREAS

1. **WORKING WITH OFFICE RECORDS:** These questions test your ability to work with office records. The test consists of two or more sets of questions, each set concerning a different problem. Typical record keeping problems might involve the organization or collation of numerical data from several sources; maintaining a record system using running balances; or completion of a table summarizing data using totals, subtotals, averages and percents.

2. **UNDERSTANDING AND INTERPRETING TABULAR MATERIAL:** These questions test your ability to understand, analyze, and use the internal logic of data presented in tabular form. You may be asked to perform tasks such as completing tables, drawing conclusions from them, analyzing data trends or interrelationships, and revising or combining data sets. The concepts of rate, ratio, and proportion are tested. Mathematical operations are simple, and computational speed is not a major factor in the test.

3. **ARITHMETIC COMPUTATION WITH CALCULATOR:** These questions test for the ability to use a calculator to do basic computations. Questions will involve addition, subtraction, multiplication and division. You may also be asked to calculate averages, to use percents, and to round an answer to the nearest whole number.

4. **UNDERSTANDING AND INTERPRETING WRITTEN MATERIAL:** These questions test for the ability to understand and interpret written material. You will be presented with brief reading passages and will be asked questions about the passages. You should base your answers to the questions **only** on what is presented in the passages and **not** on what you may happen to know about the topic.

5. **FUNDAMENTALS OF ACCOUNT KEEPING AND BOOKKEEPING:** These questions test for a knowledge of basic principles and practices of account keeping and bookkeeping. The questions test for recognizing account keeping and bookkeeping terms, concepts and relationships; recording financial transactions; and solving elementary problems in account keeping and bookkeeping.

6. **OPERATIONS WITH LETTERS AND NUMBERS**: These questions test your skills and abilities in operations involving alphabetizing, comparing, checking and counting. The questions require you to follow the specific directions given for each question which may involve alphabetizing, comparing, checking and counting given groups of letters and/or numbers.

LIST OF SUBJECT AREAS – CONTINUED

7. **PREPARING WRITTEN MATERIAL:** These questions test for the ability to present information clearly and accurately, and to organize paragraphs logically and comprehensibly. For some questions, you will be given information in two or three sentences followed by four restatements of the information. You must then choose the best version. For other questions, you will be given paragraphs with their sentences out of order. You must then choose, from four suggestions, the best order for the sentences.

8. **SUPERVISION:** These questions test for knowledge of the principles and practices employed in planning, organizing, and controlling the activities of a work unit toward predetermined objectives. The concepts covered, usually in a situational question format, include such topics as assigning and reviewing work; evaluating performance; maintaining work standards; motivating and developing subordinates; implementing procedural change; increasing efficiency; and dealing with problems of absenteeism, morale, and discipline.

9. **ADMINISTRATIVE SUPERVISION:** These questions test for knowledge of the principles and practices involved in directing the activities of a large subordinate staff, including subordinate supervisors. Questions relate to the personal interactions between an upper level supervisor and his/her subordinate supervisors in the accomplishment of objectives. These questions cover such areas as assigning work to and coordinating the activities of several units, establishing and guiding staff development programs, evaluating the performance of subordinate supervisors, and maintaining relationships with other organizational sections.

10. **NAME AND NUMBER CHECKING:** These questions test for the ability to distinguish between sets of words, letters, and/or numbers that are almost exactly alike. Material is usually presented in two or three columns, and you will have to determine how the entry in the first column compares with the entry in the second column and possibly the third. You will be instructed to mark your answers according to a designated code provided in the directions.

SUBJECT AREA 1

WORKING WITH OFFICE RECORDS: These questions test your ability to work with office records. The test consists of two or more sets of questions, each set concerning a different problem. Typical record keeping problems might involve the organization or collation of numerical data from several sources; maintaining a record system using running balances; or completion of a table summarizing data using totals, subtotals, averages and percents. **You should bring with you a hand-held battery- or solar-powered calculator for use on this test.** You will **not** be permitted to use the **calculator** function of your **cell phone.**

TEST TASKS: The test consists of two or more "sets" of questions. Each set involves a different type of problem. Some examples of typical record keeping problems are:

- the organization or collation of data from several sources
- scheduling
- maintaining a record system using running balances
- completion of a table summarizing data using totals, subtotals, averages and percents.

NOTE: Only one type of problem set is presented in this Test Guide for this subject area. The actual test may or may not have a set of this type. It will certainly have at least one set involving a different type of problem.

On the following pages are two tables, three sample questions based on the tables, and the solutions to the questions. Please look at the tables, and read both the questions and the solutions carefully.

- After each of the sample questions are four choices: for most questions, three choices are numbers and one choice is the statement, "none of the above." For these questions, once you have completed your computations, select either the choice which is the same as your answer, or, if no choice matches your answer, select "none of the above."

- Some questions have numbers for all four choices. If none of the choices matches your calculation, you have made an error, and you should recheck your work.

DIRECTIONS FOR SAMPLE QUESTIONS: Base your answers to the next three sample questions on the table, "Summary Report of Business Expenses for 2024." Complete as much of the report as you need to answer the sample questions. Use the information given in the summary report itself and in the table, "Report of Business Expenses, 3rd and 4th Quarters (26 weeks)." Both tables are shown on the following page.

SUBJECT AREA 1 - CONTINUED

REPORT OF BUSINESS EXPENSES, 3rd AND 4th QUARTERS (26 weeks)				
	3rd Quarter		4th Quarter	
	2024	2023	2024	2023
Payroll Expenses	$55,900	$47,800	$72,700	$65,100
Rental Expenses	22,500	18,900	22,500	18,900
Equipment Expenses				
New Equipment	705	375	5,575	675
Maintenance/Repair	2,860	3,000	3,140	3,400
Utility Expenses				
Electricity	4,850	4,630	4,590	4,450
Heat	130	270	440	410
Employee Benefit Expenses	18,450	15,850	24,100	21,550
Employee Contributions*	*2,500	*2,200	*3,350	*3,040
Total Net Business Expenses*		$88,625		$111,445
*NOTE: Employee Contributions are subtracted from business expenses to obtain Total Net Business Expenses				

SUMMARY REPORT OF BUSINESS EXPENSES FOR 2024							
	1st Quarter	2nd Quarter	1st Half	3rd Quarter	4th Quarter	2nd Half	Total for Year
Payroll Expenses	$81,800	$69,300	$151,100			R	
Rental Expenses	22,500	22,500	45,000				
Equipment Expenses	5,235	3,545	8,780				S
Utility Expenses	6,675	5,125	11,800				
Employee Benefit Expenses	26,900	22,900	49,800				
Employee Contributions*	*3,750	*3,200	*6,950				
Total Net Business Expenses* for 2024	139,360	120,170	259,530				
Total Net Business Expenses* for 2023			$231,780			$200,070	
% Change **			V				
*NOTE: Employee Contributions are subtracted from business expenses to obtain Total Net Business Expenses							
**NOTE: % Change is the % of increase in Total Net Business Expenses from 2023 to 2024.							

SUBJECT AREA 1 - CONTINUED

SAMPLE QUESTION 1:

What is the value of **R**?

A. $112,900
B. $128,600
C. $137,800
D. none of the above

The correct answer to this sample question is Choice B, which is $128,600.

SOLUTION: *To answer this question correctly you must calculate the value of* ***R*** *(the Payroll Expenses for the 2nd half of 2024).*

- *The Payroll Expenses for the 3rd and 4th Quarters are shown in the table, "Report of Business Expenses, 3rd and 4th Quarters (26 weeks)." (Be careful to use the amounts for 2024, and not the amounts for 2023).*

- *You must add the Payroll Expenses for the 3rd Quarter of 2024 ($55,900) to the Payroll Expenses for the 4th Quarter of 2024 ($72,700).*

- *The result is $128,600.*

SUBJECT AREA 1 - CONTINUED

SAMPLE QUESTION 2:

What is the value of **S**?

A. $ 8,780
B. $15,060
C $16,230
D. none of the above

The correct answer to this sample question is Choice D, "none of the above."

SOLUTION: *To answer this question correctly you must calculate the value of **S** (the total Equipment Expenses for the year 2024).*

- *You need to understand that Equipment Expenses are expenses for both New Equipment and for Maintenance/Repair.*

- *The Equipment Expenses for the 3rd and 4th Quarters are shown in the table, "Report of Business Expenses, 3rd and 4th Quarters (26 weeks)." (Again, be careful to use the amounts for 2024, and not the amounts for 2023.)*

- *You must add Equipment Expenses for the 3rd Quarter of 2024 ($705 + $2,860) to Equipment Expenses for the 4th Quarter of 2024 ($5,575 + $3,140) in order to calculate Equipment Expenses for the 2nd half of 2024.*

- *$705 + $2,860 + $5,575 + $3,140 = $12,280.*

- *You must then add Equipment Expenses for the 2nd half of 2024 to Equipment Expenses for the 1st half of 2024, in order to calculate Equipment Expenses for the whole year.*

- *Equipment Expenses for the 1st half of 2024 are shown in the table, "Summary Report of Business Expenses for 2024."*

- *$12,280 + 8,780 = $21,060. This is the value of **S**, the total Equipment Expenses for the year 2024.*

SAMPLE QUESTION 3:

Which one of the following is closest to the value of **V**?

A. 10%
B. 11%
C. 12%
D. 28%

The correct answer to this sample question is Choice C, which is 12%.

SOLUTION: *To answer this question correctly you must calculate the value of **V** (the percent change in Total Net Business Expenses from the 1st half of 2023 to the 1st half of 2024.*

- *You must first calculate the amount of change in Total Net Business Expenses from the 1st half of 2023 to the 1st half of 2024.*

- *Subtract the Total Net Business Expenses for the 1st half of 2023 ($231,780) from the Total Net Business Expenses for the 1st half of 2024 ($259,530).*

- *The result is $27,750.*

- *You must then calculate the percent change from the 1st half of 2023 to the 1st half of 2024. Since the percent change is from the 1st half of 2023, the basis of the comparison is the Total Net Business Expenses for the 1st half of 2023.*

- *Divide the amount of the change by the Total Net Business Expenses for the 1st half of 2023.*

- *$27,750 divided by $231,780 = .119726, or 11.9726%*

- *This is closest to 12%.*

SUBJECT AREA 2

UNDERSTANDING AND INTERPRETING TABULAR MATERIAL: These questions test your ability to understand, analyze, and use the internal logic of data presented in tabular form. You may be asked to perform tasks such as completing tables, drawing conclusions from them, analyzing data trends or interrelationships, and revising or combining data sets. The concepts of rate, ratio, and proportion are tested. Mathematical operations are simple, and computational speed is not a major factor in the test.

TEST TASK: The questions in this subject area are contained in two or more "sets." Each set consists of data presented in one or more tables, followed by a number of questions. Candidates must use the appropriate data from the table, in combination with the information given in each question, in order to answer the questions correctly.

SAMPLE TABLE:

Directions: Base your answers to the following three questions on the information in the table below.

Population of a City by Age and Gender
(In Thousands)

Age	Female	Male	Total
Under 25	70	72	142
25-34	?	27	?
35-44	?	28	53
45-54	27	28	55
55-64	30	?	57
65 and over	85	75	160
Total	261	257	518

Note: Spaces with question marks can be filled in using information given in the table and in the questions.

SAMPLE QUESTION 1:

How many people in the city were between 25 and 34 years old?

A. 51
B. 27,000
C. 51,000
D. cannot be determined from the information provided

The correct answer to this sample question is C.

SOLUTION: *To answer this question correctly, you must first note that the numbers in the table represent thousands of people (see the table heading). You are asked to find the total number of people aged 25-34. Since this information is missing from the table, it is necessary to calculate it by using other information which is in the table. You must add the number of people in all the age groups other than 25-34, and then subtract this sum from the total population of the city. This will give the number of people aged 25-34.*

142,000	*under 25*		
+53,000	*35-44*	*518,000*	*total population (all ages)*
+55,000	*45-54*	*- 467,000*	*total population (all ages except 25-34)*
+57,000	*55-64*	*51,000*	*population aged 25-34*
+160,000	*65 and over*		
467,000			

There are 51,000 people in the city between the ages of 25 and 34 (choice C).

SAMPLE QUESTION 2:

Most nearly what percent of the total population of the city was female aged 35 to 54?

A. 5%
B. 10%
C. 14%
D. 20%

The correct answer to sample question 2 is B.

SOLUTION: *To answer this question correctly you must find the number of females aged 35 to 54. This requires you to add the number of females aged 35-44 to the number aged 45-54. You must first find the number of females who are aged 35 to 44. This information is missing from the table, but you can calculate it by subtracting the number of males who are aged 35 to 44 from the total number of people in that age group.*

(53,000 – 28,000 = 25,000; there are 25,000 females aged 35-44).

You then need to add the number of females aged 35-44 to the number of females aged 45-54;

(25,000 + 27,000 = 52,000; there are 52,000 females between the ages of 35 and 54).

You must then divide this number by the total population of the city, and convert the answer to a percent.

(52,000/518,000 = .100386; ***this is nearest to 10%****).*

Therefore, the percentage of the total population of the city which was female aged 35 to 54 is 10% (choice B).

SUBJECT AREA 2 - CONTINUED

SAMPLE QUESTION 3:

If 40% of the total male population of the city earns wages, and 30% of the total female population of the city earns wages, which one of the following statements comparing the number of males earning wages to the number of females earning wages is true?

A. There are 24,500 more males than females earning wages.
B. There are 27,300 more males than females earning wages.
C. There are 51,800 more males than females earning wages.
D. There are 27,300 fewer males than females earning wages.

The correct answer to sample question 3 is A.

SOLUTION: *To answer this question correctly you must use some information given in the question and some information given in the table. It is important to be careful and apply the correct percentage for each gender. (The percentage for males is given first in the question, but the number of males is second in the table).*

To calculate the number of males earning wages, multiply the total number of males by 40%. (257,000 x .40 = 102,800)

To calculate the number of females earning wages, multiply the total number of females by 30%. (261,000 x .30 = 78,300)

To compare the two numbers, subtract the number of female wage earners from the number of male wage earners. (102,800 – 78,300 = 24,500)

There are 24,500 more male wage earners than female wage earners (choice A).

SUBJECT AREA 3

ARITHMETIC COMPUTATION WITH CALCULATOR: These questions test for the ability to use a calculator to do basic computations. Questions will involve addition, subtraction, multiplication and division. You may also be asked to calculate averages, to use percents, and to round an answer to the nearest whole number. **You should bring with you a hand-held battery- or solar-powered calculator for use on this test.** You will **not** be permitted to use the **calculator** function of your **cell phone.**

TEST TASKS: Each question has three separate computational problems. You must solve each problem and then add the three answers together (this is the SUM).

- For some questions you will need to **round** the SUM to the nearest whole number. (See SAMPLE QUESTION 1 on the next page.)

- For other questions you will need to find the AVERAGE of the three answers, by dividing the SUM by three. Then you will need to **round** the AVERAGE to the nearest whole number. (See SAMPLE QUESTION 2.)

- For some other questions, you will need to find a PERCENT of the SUM. Then you will need to **round** the PERCENT of the SUM to the nearest whole number. (See SAMPLE QUESTION 3.)

After each question are four choices: three choices are whole numbers and one choice is the statement, "none of the above."

Once you have completed your computations, select either the choice which is the same as your answer, or, if no choice matches your answer, select "none of the above".

On the following pages are three sample questions and the solutions to the questions. Please read both the questions and the solutions carefully.

Note: To round to the nearest whole number you only have to look at the digit after the decimal point. If it is less than 5, round down – drop the digits after the decimal point. If the digit after the decimal point is 5 or greater, round up to the next higher whole number. (NOTE: A whole number has no decimals or fractions.)

See the Sample Questions and Solutions on the following pages.

SUBJECT AREA 3 - CONTINUED

DIRECTIONS FOR SAMPLE QUESTION 1: The next question lists three separate computational problems. Solve each problem, then add the three answers together (this is the SUM). ROUND the SUM to the nearest whole number.

Note: A calculator would be helpful when performing the computations.

SAMPLE QUESTION 1:

Multiply: 240 by 152.4 =
Divide: 49,362 by 142.5 =
Add: 1,218 plus 8,052.3 plus 89.62 =

The SUM of the answers to the three problems above, ROUNDED to the nearest whole number, is

A. 46,282
B. 46,362
C. 47,928
D. none of the above

The correct answer to this sample question is Choice ***A,*** *which is 46,282.*

SOLUTION: *To answer this question correctly, first you must solve each problem in order. Then, you must add the three answers together. Finally, you must round the added total (SUM) to the nearest whole number.*

- ***Multiply*** *240 by 152.4;* ***the result is 36,576****.*
- ***Divide*** *49,362 by 142.5;* ***the result is 346.4****.*
- ***Add*** *1,218 plus 8,052.3 plus 89.62;* ***the result is 9,359.92****.*

Add the three answers together*: 36,576 plus 346.4 plus 9,359.92; the result is* ***46,282.32****.*

Round *46,282.32 to the nearest whole number;* ***the result is 46,282****.*

Note: *To round to the nearest whole number you only have to look at the digit after the decimal point. If it is less than 5, round down —drop the digits after the decimal point. If the digit after the decimal point is 5 or greater, round up to the next higher whole number. (NOTE: A whole number has no decimals or fractions.)*

To round 46,282.32 to the nearest whole number, look at the digit after the decimal point; the digit is 3. Since 3 is less than 5, the nearest whole number to 46,282.32 is ***46,282****. (If the sum of the answers to the three problems had been 46,282.5 or 46,282.6, etc., the nearest whole number would have been 46,283.)*

NOTE: If the ROUNDED SUM is not one of the ***A****,* ***B*** *or* ***C*** *choices listed, the answer would be choice D, "none of the above."*

SUBJECT AREA 3 - CONTINUED

DIRECTIONS FOR SAMPLE QUESTION 2: The next question lists three separate computational problems. **Solve** each problem, **add** the three answers together (this is the SUM), and then **divide** the SUM by 3 to find the AVERAGE of the three answers. ROUND the AVERAGE to the nearest whole number.

Note: A calculator would be helpful when performing the computations.

SAMPLE QUESTION 2:

Divide:	Subtract:	Add:
8746.3 ÷149	12,572.5 - 896.94	98,017 plus 7,542.3 plus 79,188.63

The AVERAGE of the answers to the three problems above, ROUNDED to the nearest whole number, is

A. 65,474
B. 65,494
C. 196,482
D. none of the above

*The correct answer to this sample question is Choice **B,** which is 65,494.*

SOLUTION: *To answer this question correctly, you must solve each problem in order. Add the three answers together (this is the SUM). Then divide the SUM by 3 to get the AVERAGE of the three answers. Finally, you must round the AVERAGE to the nearest whole number.*

- ***Divide** 8,746.3 by 149; **the result is 58.7***
- ***Subtract** 896.94 from 12,572.5; **the result is 11,675.56***
- ***Add** 98,017 + 7,542.3 + 79,188.63; **the result is 184,747.93***
- Add the three answers together: 58.7+11,675.56+184,747.93; the result is 196,482.19
- ***Divide** 196,482.19 by 3 to get the AVERAGE; **the result is 65,494.063***
- ***Round** 65,494.063 the nearest whole number; **the result is 65,494** (Look at the digit after the decimal point; the digit is 0. Since 0 is less than 5, round down — drop the digits after the decimal point. The nearest whole number to 65,494.063 is **65,494**.)*

*NOTE: If the ROUNDED AVERAGE is not one of the **A**, **B** or **C** choices listed, the answer would be choice **D**, "none of the above."*

DIRECTIONS FOR SAMPLE QUESTION 3: The next question lists three separate computational problems. Solve each problem, add the three answers together (this is the SUM), and then find the indicated PERCENT (%) of the SUM of the three answers. ROUND the PERCENT of the SUM of the three answers to the nearest whole number.

Note: A calculator would be helpful when performing the computations.

SAMPLE QUESTION 3:

Multiply: one-fourth x 6,241.7

Add: 1,873.5
+ 31,409.04

Divide: 73,091.72 by 238.55

Twenty eight percent (28%) of the SUM of the answers to the three problems above, ROUNDED to the nearest whole number is

A. 9,822
B. 16,396
C. 98,418
D. none of the above

*The correct answer to this sample question is Choice **D,** "none of the above."*

SOLUTION: *To answer this question correctly, you must solve each problem in order. Add the three answers together (this is the SUM). Then multiply the SUM by twenty eight percent (28%, or .28). Finally, you must round 28% of the SUM to the nearest whole number.*

- ***Multiply*** *one-fourth (one divided by four, or .25) by 6,241.7;* ***the result is 1,560.425***
- ***Add*** *1,873.5 + 31,409.04;* ***the result is 33,282.54***
- ***Divide*** *73,091.72 by 238.55;* ***the result is 306.4***
- ***Add the three answers together:*** *1,560.425 + 33,282.54 + 306.4;* ***The result is 35,149.365***
- ***Multiply*** *35,149.365 by 28% (.28);* ***the result is 9,841.822***
- ***Round*** *9,841.822 to the nearest whole number;* ***the result is 9,842 (****Look at the digit after the decimal point; the digit is 8. Since 8 is greater than 5, round up —go to the next highest whole number. The nearest whole number to 9,841.822 is* ***9,842****.)*

SUBJECT AREA 4

UNDERSTANDING AND INTERPRETING WRITTEN MATERIAL: These questions test for the ability to understand and interpret written material. You will be presented with brief reading passages and will be asked questions about the passages. You should base your answers to the questions **only** on what is presented in the passages and **not** on what you may happen to know about the topic.

TEST TASK: You will be provided with brief reading passages and then will be asked questions relating to the passages. All the information required to answer the questions will be provided in the passages.

SAMPLE QUESTION:

"Increasingly, behavior termed 'road rage' is being viewed as a public health issue, because of the number of deaths and injuries related to it. Such behavior is often a reaction to the feeling that one has been treated unfairly by another driver, and it is much less likely to occur if a driver is treated fairly. 'Fair play' on the road includes the observance not only of traffic regulations but also of the rules of courtesy. Courteous driving is based on common sense consideration for other drivers and a strong desire to make the roads safe for everyone. Good highway manners should become just as much a matter of habit as other kinds of manners."

Which one of the following statements is best supported by the above selection?

A. Courteous driving contributes to road safety.
B. Those who are generally polite are also courteous drivers.
C. Unlike driving courtesy, the observance of traffic regulations is a matter of habit.
D. Being courteous when driving is more important than observing traffic regulations.

The correct answer to this sample question is A.

SOLUTION: To answer this question correctly, you must evaluate each choice against the written selection and determine the one that is best supported by the written selection.

***Choice A** states, "Courteous driving contributes to road safety." Choice A is supported by the statement in the written selection that, "Courteous driving is based on...a strong desire to make the roads safe for everyone." This is the correct answer.*

***Choice B** states, "Those who are generally polite are also courteous drivers." Choice B is not supported by the written selection. The written selection does not mention "those who are generally polite" at all. Choice B is not the correct answer to this question.*

***Choice C** states, "Unlike driving courtesy, the observance of traffic regulations is a matter of habit." Choice C is not supported by the written selection. The written selection makes no such bold statement. Instead, the written material mildly suggests that "Good highway manners should become just as much a matter of habit as other kinds of manners." Choice C is not the correct answer to this question.*

***Choice D** states, "Being courteous when driving is more important than observing traffic regulations." Choice D is not supported by the written selection. The written selection states, "'Fair play' on the road includes the observance not only of traffic regulations but also of the rules of courtesy." The written selection does not state that being courteous is more important than observing traffic regulations. Choice D is not the correct answer to this question.*

SUBJECT AREA 5

FUNDAMENTALS OF ACCOUNT KEEPING AND BOOKKEEPING: These questions test for a knowledge of basic principles and practices of account keeping and bookkeeping. The questions test for recognizing account keeping and bookkeeping terms, concepts and relationships; recording financial transactions; and solving elementary problems in account keeping and bookkeeping.

TEST TASK: You will be presented with questions that test for knowledge of the more elementary aspects of bookkeeping and accounting. To answer these questions, you will need basic knowledge of double-entry bookkeeping and concepts such as depreciation, assets, liabilities, books of account, balance sheets, and accounting cycles.

SAMPLE QUESTION 1:

An agency purchases office equipment for $7,000. The agency pays with cash. Which one of the following entries correctly records this transaction?

A. Dr. Office equipment $7,000
    Cr. Cash $7,000
B. Dr. Cash $7,000
    Cr. Office equipment $7,000
C. Dr. Office equipment $7,000
    Cr. Accounts payable $7,000
D. Dr. Accounts payable $7,000
    Cr. Office equipment $7,000

The correct answer to this sample question is choice A.

SOLUTION: *To answer this question correctly, you need to know that cash and office equipment are classified as assets, that increases in assets are recorded as debits, and that decreases in assets are recorded as credits. You also need to know that "accounts payable" is a liability and that the "accounts payable" account is used to record transactions for which money is owed, such as if the office equipment had been purchased on credit.*

In this question, the asset office equipment increases by $7,000, so the transaction is recorded as a debit to the "office equipment" account. The asset cash decreases by $7,000, so the transaction is recorded as a credit to the "cash" account. Because the office equipment was paid for in cash, no change to the "accounts payable" account resulted from this transaction.

SUBJECT AREA 5 - CONTINUED

SAMPLE QUESTION 2:

Which one of the following best defines a general journal?

A. It is a record that contains an account for each supplier that an organization does business with and owes money to for services or merchandise received.
B. It is a record that contains all the accounts used by the organization.
C. It is a record that lists transactions in the order in which they occurred and identified as either a debit or credit.
D. It is a record that lists all transactions involving the receipt of cash.

The correct answer to this sample question is choice C.

SOLUTION: *To answer this question correctly, you need to know the difference between journals and ledgers and the purpose each one serves. Journals are used to keep track of transactions. Ledgers are organized by accounts. Choice A describes an accounts payable ledger. Choice B describes a general ledger. Choice D describes a cash receipts journal. Choice C describes a general journal.*

SUBJECT AREA 6

OPERATIONS WITH LETTERS AND NUMBERS: These questions test for the ability to alphabetize, compare, check, and count groups of letters and/or numbers.

TEST TASK: Each question involves a variety of operations with letters and numbers. Your task will be to determine the correct answer by alphabetizing, comparing, checking, and/or counting a given group of letters and/or numbers.

SAMPLE QUESTION 1:

Which one of the following letters is as far after C in the alphabet as T is after O?

A. G
B. H
C. I
D. J

The correct answer to Sample Question 1 is Choice B.

SOLUTION TO SAMPLE QUESTION 1: *To answer this question correctly, you must first count the number of letters that fall between O and T in the alphabet. There are four such letters (P, Q, R, S). You must then count four letters from C (D, E, F, G), and then identify the next letter, H.* ***Since the letter H is as far after C in the alphabet as T is after O.***

SAMPLE QUESTION 2:

In the following list of numbers, how many times does 8 come just after 6 when 6 comes just after an odd number?

6325687253494236844576842396868

A. 2
B. 3
C. 4
D. 5

The correct answer to Sample Question 2 is Choice C.

SOLUTION TO SAMPLE QUESTION 2: *To answer this question correctly, you must read the list of numbers from left to right and:*

- *locate each 8 that comes just after a 6 in the list of numbers given in the problem*
- *determine whether the 6 comes just after an odd number*
- *count how many occasions where 8 comes just after a 6 that comes just after an odd number*

In this problem, there are ***4 occasions*** *where 8 comes just after a 6 that comes just after an odd number (568, 368, 768, 968).* ***Since 8 comes just after 6 when 6 comes just after an odd number a total of 4 times.***

SUBJECT AREA 7

PREPARING WRITTEN MATERIAL: These questions test for the ability to present information clearly and accurately, and to organize paragraphs logically and comprehensibly. For some questions, you will be given information in two or three sentences followed by four restatements of the information. You must then choose the best version. For other questions, you will be given paragraphs with their sentences out of order. You must then choose, from four suggestions, the best order for the sentences.

TEST TASK: There are two separate test tasks in this subject area.

For the first, **Information Presentation**, you will be given information in two or three sentences, followed by four restatements of the information. You must then choose the best version. There will be ten Information Presentation questions on the multiple-choice test.

For the second, **Paragraph Organization**, you will be given paragraphs with their sentences out of order, and then be asked to choose, from among four suggestions, the best order for the sentences. There will be five Paragraph Organization questions on the multiple-choice test.

INFORMATION PRESENTATION SAMPLE QUESTION:

Martin Wilson failed to take proper precautions. His failure to take proper precautions caused a personal injury accident.

Which one of the following best presents the information above?

A. Martin Wilson failed to take proper precautions that caused a personal injury accident.
B. Proper precautions, which Martin Wilson failed to take, caused a personal injury accident.
C. Martin Wilson's failure to take proper precautions caused a personal injury accident.
D. Martin Wilson, who failed to take proper precautions, was in a personal injury accident.

The best answer to this sample question is C.

SOLUTION:

Choice A *conveys the incorrect impression that proper precautions caused a personal injury accident.*

Choice B *conveys the incorrect impression that proper precautions caused a personal injury accident.*

Choice C *best presents the original information: Martin Wilson failed to take proper precautions, and this failure caused a personal injury accident.*

Choice D *states that Martin Wilson was in a personal injury accident. The original information states that Martin Wilson caused a personal injury accident, but it does not state that Martin Wilson was in a personal injury accident.*

PARAGRAPH ORGANIZATION SAMPLE QUESTION:

The following question is based upon a group of sentences. The sentences are shown out of sequence, but when correctly arranged, they form a connected, well-organized paragraph. Read the sentences, and then answer the question about the best arrangement of these sentences.

1. Eventually, they piece all of this information together and make a choice.
2. Before actually deciding upon a human services job, people usually think about several possibilities.
3. They imagine themselves in different situations, and in so doing, they probably think about their interests, goals, and abilities.
4. Choosing among occupations in the field of human services is an important decision to make.

Which one of the following is the best arrangement of these sentences?

A. 2-4-1-3
B. 2-3-4-1
C. 4-2-1-3
D. 4-2-3-1

The best answer to this sample question is D.

SOLUTION:

***Choices A and C** present the information in the paragraph out of logical sequence. In both **A** and **C**, sentence 1 comes before sentence 3. The key element in the organization of this paragraph is that sentence 3 contains the information to which sentence 1 refers; therefore, in logical sequence, sentence 3 should come before sentence 1.*

***Choice B** also presents the information in the paragraph out of logical sequence. Choice **B** places sentence 4 in between sentence 1 and sentence 3, thereby interrupting the logical sequence of the information in the paragraph.*

***Choice D** presents the information in the paragraph in the best logical sequence. Sentence 4 introduces the main idea of the paragraph: "choosing an occupation in the field of human services." Sentences 2-3-1 then follow up on this idea by describing, in order, the steps involved in making such a choice. Choice **D** is the best answer to this sample question.*

SUBJECT AREA 8

SUPERVISION: These questions test for knowledge of the principles and practices employed in planning, organizing, and controlling the activities of a work unit toward predetermined objectives. The concepts covered, usually in a situational question format, include such topics as assigning and reviewing work; evaluating performance; maintaining work standards; motivating and developing subordinates; implementing procedural change; increasing efficiency; and dealing with problems of absenteeism, morale, and discipline.

TEST TASK: You will be presented with situations in which you must apply knowledge of supervisory principles and practices in order to answer the question correctly.

SAMPLE QUESTION:

Assume the unit you supervise is given a new work assignment and that you are unsure about the proper procedure to use in performing this assignment. Which one of the following actions should you take first in this situation?

A. Obtain input from your staff.
B. Consult other unit supervisors who have had similar assignments.
C. Use an appropriate procedure from a similar assignment that you are familiar with.
D. Discuss the matter with your supervisor.

The correct answer to this sample question is D.

SOLUTION: This question asks for the action that you should take FIRST in this situation.

***Choice A** is not correct. Since this assignment is new for your unit, your staff would not be expected to be more knowledgeable than you about the proper procedure.*

***Choice B** is not correct. Although discussing this matter with other supervisors may increase your knowledge of the new assignment, similar assignments performed in other units may differ in some important way from your new assignment. Other units may also function differently from your unit, so the procedures used to perform similar assignments may differ accordingly.*

***Choice C** is not correct. Since this assignment is new for your unit, you would have no way of knowing whether the procedure from a similar assignment is appropriate to use. You would need someone with the appropriate knowledge, usually your supervisor, to determine if the procedure from a similar assignment could be used before you actually employed this procedure in the performance of your new assignment.*

***Choice D is the correct answer to this question.** Your supervisor is more likely to be informed about what procedure may be appropriate for work that he or she assigns to you than would other unit supervisors or your staff. Even if your supervisor does not know what procedure is appropriate, a decision regarding which procedure to use should be made with his or her participation, since he or she has the ultimate responsibility for your unit's work.*

SUBJECT AREA 9

ADMINISTRATIVE SUPERVISION: These questions test for knowledge of the principles and practices involved in directing the activities of a large subordinate staff, including subordinate supervisors. Questions relate to the personal interactions between an upper level supervisor and his/her subordinate supervisors in the accomplishment of objectives. These questions cover such areas as assigning work to and coordinating the activities of several units, establishing and guiding staff development programs, evaluating the performance of subordinate supervisors, and maintaining relationships with other organizational sections.

TEST TASK: You will be presented with situations in which you must apply knowledge of the principles and practices of administrative supervision to answer the questions correctly. You will be placed in the role of a supervisor of a section, which is made up of several units. Each unit has a supervisor and several employees. All unit supervisors report directly to you.

SAMPLE QUESTION:

You have delegated a work project to two unit supervisors and have asked them to collaborate on it. Later, you observe two employees strongly arguing about which one of them is responsible for a certain activity within the work project. The arguing employees work for different units. Which one of the following actions is most appropriate for you to take in this situation?

A. Intercede in the employees' argument and settle it.
B. Meet with the unit supervisors of the two employees and inform them of the situation you observed.
C. Inform one unit supervisor of the situation and ask this supervisor to take care of it.
D. Set up a meeting that includes both unit supervisors and both employees to resolve the situation.

The correct answer to this sample question is B.

SOLUTION:

Choice A *is not correct. In your position, you supervise properly by giving direction through your unit supervisors. By taking this choice, you are not allowing your unit supervisors to handle a problem involving their staff members. Also, it is not reasonable that you would be able to settle the employees' dispute. Earlier, you delegated the work project to the two unit supervisors, who would be responsible for assigning activities related to the project. The two unit supervisors must deal with the problem.*

Choice B is the correct answer to this question. *The two unit supervisors are collaborating on the work project and therefore giving the assignments. You should meet with them and tell them about the employees' argument. The unit supervisors should be informed about the point of contention and the fact that the two employees had a heated argument. The unit supervisors must then work out a way to handle the situation.*

The solution to the above Sample Question is continued on the next page.

SOLUTION: (Continued)

Choice C *is not correct. Speaking to only one supervisor about the situation means that the second supervisor may be uninformed, or only partly informed, about the situation. You cannot be assured that the first supervisor will include the second supervisor in finding a way to settle the issue. If the first unit supervisor chooses to handle the situation on his own and speak to both employees, this supervisor would be giving direction to one employee from another unit. This is not good supervisory practice. Also, in taking Choice C, you are favoring one supervisor and slighting the other.*

Choice D *is not correct. The unit supervisors need to come up with a way of handling the situation that you observed. To do this, they must be informed without the employees present. Also, by including the employees in the meeting, you may get a replay of their earlier argument, which is not helpful.*

SUBJECT AREA 10

NAME AND NUMBER CHECKING: These questions test for the ability to distinguish between sets of words, letters, and/or numbers that are almost exactly alike. Material is usually presented in two or three columns, and you will have to determine how the entry in the first column compares with the entry in the second column and possibly the third. You will be instructed to mark your answers according to a designated code provided in the directions.

TEST TASK: You will be asked to determine if the information is the same or different in each of three sets.

Directions: Each of the questions consists of a set of information written three times. Compare the three sets in each question and on your answer sheet mark:

Compare the three sets of information given in each question; then select:

Choice A - *if only the first and second sets are exactly alike*
Choice B - *if only the first and third sets are exactly alike*
Choice C - *if only the second and third sets are exactly alike*
Choice D - *if no two sets are exactly alike*

SAMPLE QUESTION 1:

Set 1	Set 2	Set 3
Fruchter, William	Fruchter, William	Fruchter, William
543 Peter Avenue	543 Peter Avenue	543 Peter Avenue
Potsdam, N.Y. 12435	Potsdam, N.Y. 12345	Potsdam, N.Y. 12435
809-43-4537	809-43-4537	809-43-4537
5' 10" 170 lbs. GR	5' 10" 170 lbs. GR	5' 10" 170 lbs. GR

SOLUTION: *The zip code in the third line of the second set is 12345. The zip code in the third line of the first and third sets is 12435. The information given in the first and third sets is exactly alike; therefore, the correct answer is B.*

Sample Question 2 is on the following page.

SUBJECT AREA 10 – CONTINUED

NAME AND NUMBER CHECKING

SAMPLE QUESTION 2:

Set 1	**Set 2**	**Set 3**
Gonzalez, Sharon	Gonzalez, Sharon	Gonzales, Sharon
54 Laird Drive	54 Laird Road	54 Laird Drive
Hartford, NY 13413	Hartford, NY 13413	Hartford, NY 13413
160-40-6973	160-40-6973	160-40-6973
4' 11" 110 lbs. BR	4' 11" 110 lbs. BR	4' 11" 110 lbs. BR

SOLUTION: *The name in sets 1 and 2 is Gonzale**z**; in set 3, the name is Gonzale**s**. The address in sets 1 and 3 is 54 Laird **Drive**; in set 2, the address is 54 Laird **Road.** Since no two sets are exactly alike, the correct answer to sample question 2 is Choice **D**.*

HOW TO TAKE A TEST

I. YOU MUST PASS AN EXAMINATION

A. WHAT EVERY CANDIDATE SHOULD KNOW

Examination applicants often ask us for help in preparing for the written test. What can I study in advance? What kinds of questions will be asked? How will the test be given? How will the papers be graded?

As an applicant for a civil service examination, you may be wondering about some of these things. Our purpose here is to suggest effective methods of advance study and to describe civil service examinations.

Your chances for success on this examination can be increased if you know how to prepare. Those "pre-examination jitters" can be reduced if you know what to expect. You can even experience an adventure in good citizenship if you know why civil service exams are given.

B. WHY ARE CIVIL SERVICE EXAMINATIONS GIVEN?

Civil service examinations are important to you in two ways. As a citizen, you want public jobs filled by employees who know how to do their work. As a job seeker, you want a fair chance to compete for that job on an equal footing with other candidates. The best-known means of accomplishing this two-fold goal is the competitive examination.

Exams are widely publicized throughout the nation. They may be administered for jobs in federal, state, city, municipal, town or village governments or agencies.

Any citizen may apply, with some limitations, such as the age or residence of applicants. Your experience and education may be reviewed to see whether you meet the requirements for the particular examination. When these requirements exist, they are reasonable and applied consistently to all applicants. Thus, a competitive examination may cause you some uneasiness now, but it is your privilege and safeguard.

C. HOW ARE CIVIL SERVICE EXAMS DEVELOPED?

Examinations are carefully written by trained technicians who are specialists in the field known as "psychological measurement," in consultation with recognized authorities in the field of work that the test will cover. These experts recommend the subject matter areas or skills to be tested; only those knowledges or skills important to your success on the job are included. The most reliable books and source materials available are used as references. Together, the experts and technicians judge the difficulty level of the questions.

Test technicians know how to phrase questions so that the problem is clearly stated. Their ethics do not permit "trick" or "catch" questions. Questions may have been tried out on sample groups, or subjected to statistical analysis, to determine their usefulness.

Written tests are often used in combination with performance tests, ratings of training and experience, and oral interviews. All of these measures combine to form the best-known means of finding the right person for the right job.

II. HOW TO PASS THE WRITTEN TEST

A. NATURE OF THE EXAMINATION

To prepare intelligently for civil service examinations, you should know how they differ from school examinations you have taken. In school you were assigned certain definite pages to read or subjects to cover. The examination questions were quite detailed and usually emphasized memory. Civil service exams, on the other hand, try to discover your present ability to perform the duties of a position, plus your potentiality to learn these duties. In other words, a civil service exam attempts to predict how successful you will be. Questions cover such a broad area that they cannot be as minute and detailed as school exam questions.

In the public service similar kinds of work, or positions, are grouped together in one "class." This process is known as *position-classification.* All the positions in a class are paid according to the salary range for that class. One class title covers all of these positions, and they are all tested by the same examination.

B. FOUR BASIC STEPS

1) Study the announcement

How, then, can you know what subjects to study? Our best answer is: "Learn as much as possible about the class of positions for which you've applied." The exam will test the knowledge, skills and abilities needed to do the work.

Your most valuable source of information about the position you want is the official exam announcement. This announcement lists the training and experience qualifications. Check these standards and apply only if you come reasonably close to meeting them.

The brief description of the position in the examination announcement offers some clues to the subjects which will be tested. Think about the job itself. Review the duties in your mind. Can you perform them, or are there some in which you are rusty? Fill in the blank spots in your preparation.

Many jurisdictions preview the written test in the exam announcement by including a section called "Knowledge and Abilities Required," "Scope of the Examination," or some similar heading. Here you will find out specifically what fields will be tested.

2) Review your own background

Once you learn in general what the position is all about, and what you need to know to do the work, ask yourself which subjects you already know fairly well and which need improvement. You may wonder whether to concentrate on improving your strong areas or on building some background in your fields of weakness. When the announcement has specified "some knowledge" or "considerable knowledge," or has used adjectives like "beginning principles of..." or "advanced ... methods," you can get a clue as to the number and difficulty of questions to be asked in any given field. More questions, and hence broader coverage, would be included for those subjects which are more important in the work. Now weigh your strengths and weaknesses against the job requirements and prepare accordingly.

3) Determine the level of the position

Another way to tell how intensively you should prepare is to understand the level of the job for which you are applying. Is it the entering level? In other words, is this the position in which beginners in a field of work are hired? Or is it an intermediate or advanced level? Sometimes this is indicated by such words as "Junior" or "Senior" in the class title. Other jurisdictions use Roman numerals to designate the level – Clerk I, Clerk II, for example. The word "Supervisor" sometimes appears in the title. If the level is not indicated by the title, check the description of duties. Will you be working under very close supervision, or will you have responsibility for independent decisions in this work?

4) Choose appropriate study materials

Now that you know the subjects to be examined and the relative amount of each subject to be covered, you can choose suitable study materials. For beginning level jobs, or even advanced ones, if you have a pronounced weakness in some aspect of your training, read a modern, standard textbook in that field. Be sure it is up to date and has general coverage. Such books are normally available at your library, and the librarian will be glad to help you locate one. For entry-level positions, questions of appropriate difficulty are chosen – neither highly advanced questions, nor those too simple. Such questions require careful thought but not advanced training.

If the position for which you are applying is technical or advanced, you will read more advanced, specialized material. If you are already familiar with the basic principles of your field, elementary textbooks would waste your time. Concentrate on advanced textbooks and technical periodicals. Think through the concepts and review difficult problems in your field.

These are all general sources. You can get more ideas on your own initiative, following these leads. For example, training manuals and publications of the government agency which employs workers in your field can be useful, particularly for technical and professional positions. A letter or visit to the government department involved may result in more specific study suggestions, and certainly will provide you with a more definite idea of the exact nature of the position you are seeking.

III. KINDS OF TESTS

Tests are used for purposes other than measuring knowledge and ability to perform specified duties. For some positions, it is equally important to test ability to make adjustments to new situations or to profit from training. In others, basic mental abilities not dependent on information are essential. Questions which test these things may not appear as pertinent to the duties of the position as those which test for knowledge and information. Yet they are often highly important parts of a fair examination. For very general questions, it is almost impossible to help you direct your study efforts. What we can do is to point out some of the more common of these general abilities needed in public service positions and describe some typical questions.

1) General information

Broad, general information has been found useful for predicting job success in some kinds of work. This is tested in a variety of ways, from vocabulary lists to questions about current events. Basic background in some field of work, such as sociology or economics, may be sampled in a group of questions. Often these are principles which have become familiar to most persons through exposure rather than through formal training. It is difficult to advise you how to study for these questions; being alert to the world around you is our best suggestion.

2) Verbal ability

An example of an ability needed in many positions is verbal or language ability. Verbal ability is, in brief, the ability to use and understand words. Vocabulary and grammar tests are typical measures of this ability. Reading comprehension or paragraph interpretation questions are common in many kinds of civil service tests. You are given a paragraph of written material and asked to find its central meaning.

3) Numerical ability

Number skills can be tested by the familiar arithmetic problem, by checking paired lists of numbers to see which are alike and which are different, or by interpreting charts and graphs. In the latter test, a graph may be printed in the test booklet which you are asked to use as the basis for answering questions.

4) Observation

A popular test for law-enforcement positions is the observation test. A picture is shown to you for several minutes, then taken away. Questions about the picture test your ability to observe both details and larger elements.

5) Following directions

In many positions in the public service, the employee must be able to carry out written instructions dependably and accurately. You may be given a chart with several columns, each column listing a variety of information. The questions require you to carry out directions involving the information given in the chart.

6) Skills and aptitudes

Performance tests effectively measure some manual skills and aptitudes. When the skill is one in which you are trained, such as typing or shorthand, you can practice. These tests are often very much like those given in business school or high school courses. For many of the other skills and aptitudes, however, no short-time preparation can be made. Skills and abilities natural to you or that you have developed throughout your lifetime are being tested.

Many of the general questions just described provide all the data needed to answer the questions and ask you to use your reasoning ability to find the answers. Your best preparation for these tests, as well as for tests of facts and ideas, is to be at your physical and mental best. You, no doubt, have your own methods of getting into an exam-taking mood and keeping "in shape." The next section lists some ideas on this subject.

IV. KINDS OF QUESTIONS

Only rarely is the "essay" question, which you answer in narrative form, used in civil service tests. Civil service tests are usually of the short-answer type. Full instructions for answering these questions will be given to you at the examination. But in case this is your first experience with short-answer questions and separate answer sheets, here is what you need to know:

1) Multiple-choice Questions

Most popular of the short-answer questions is the "multiple choice" or "best answer" question. It can be used, for example, to test for factual knowledge, ability to solve problems or judgment in meeting situations found at work.

A multiple-choice question is normally one of three types—

- It can begin with an incomplete statement followed by several possible endings. You are to find the one ending which *best* completes the statement, although some of the others may not be entirely wrong.
- It can also be a complete statement in the form of a question which is answered by choosing one of the statements listed.

- It can be in the form of a problem – again you select the best answer.

Here is an example of a multiple-choice question with a discussion which should give you some clues as to the method for choosing the right answer:

When an employee has a complaint about his assignment, the action which will *best* help him overcome his difficulty is to

A. discuss his difficulty with his coworkers
B. take the problem to the head of the organization
C. take the problem to the person who gave him the assignment
D. say nothing to anyone about his complaint

In answering this question, you should study each of the choices to find which is best. Consider choice "A" – Certainly an employee may discuss his complaint with fellow employees, but no change or improvement can result, and the complaint remains unresolved. Choice "B" is a poor choice since the head of the organization probably does not know what assignment you have been given, and taking your problem to him is known as "going over the head" of the supervisor. The supervisor, or person who made the assignment, is the person who can clarify it or correct any injustice. Choice "C" is, therefore, correct. To say nothing, as in choice "D," is unwise. Supervisors have and interest in knowing the problems employees are facing, and the employee is seeking a solution to his problem.

2) True/False Questions

The "true/false" or "right/wrong" form of question is sometimes used. Here a complete statement is given. Your job is to decide whether the statement is right or wrong.

SAMPLE: A roaming cell-phone call to a nearby city costs less than a non-roaming call to a distant city.

This statement is wrong, or false, since roaming calls are more expensive.

This is not a complete list of all possible question forms, although most of the others are variations of these common types. You will always get complete directions for answering questions. Be sure you understand *how* to mark your answers – ask questions until you do.

V. RECORDING YOUR ANSWERS

Computer terminals are used more and more today for many different kinds of exams.

For an examination with very few applicants, you may be told to record your answers in the test booklet itself. Separate answer sheets are much more common. If this separate answer sheet is to be scored by machine – and this is often the case – it is highly important that you mark your answers correctly in order to get credit.

An electronic scoring machine is often used in civil service offices because of the speed with which papers can be scored. Machine-scored answer sheets must be marked with a pencil, which will be given to you. This pencil has a high graphite content which responds to the electronic scoring machine. As a matter of fact, stray dots may register as answers, so do not let your pencil rest on the answer sheet while you are pondering the correct answer. Also, if your pencil lead breaks or is otherwise defective, ask for another.

Since the answer sheet will be dropped in a slot in the scoring machine, be careful not to bend the corners or get the paper crumpled.

The answer sheet normally has five vertical columns of numbers, with 30 numbers to a column. These numbers correspond to the question numbers in your test booklet. After each number, going across the page are four or five pairs of dotted lines. These short dotted lines have small letters or numbers above them. The first two pairs may also have a "T" or "F" above the letters. This indicates that the first two pairs only are to be used if the questions are of the true-false type. If the questions are multiple choice, disregard the "T" and "F" and pay attention only to the small letters or numbers.

Answer your questions in the manner of the sample that follows:

32. The largest city in the United States is
    A. Washington, D.C.
    B. New York City
    C. Chicago
    D. Detroit
    E. San Francisco

1) Choose the answer you think is best. (New York City is the largest, so "B" is correct.)
2) Find the row of dotted lines numbered the same as the question you are answering. (Find row number 32)
3) Find the pair of dotted lines corresponding to the answer. (Find the pair of lines under the mark "B.")
4) Make a solid black mark between the dotted lines.

VI. BEFORE THE TEST

Common sense will help you find procedures to follow to get ready for an examination. Too many of us, however, overlook these sensible measures. Indeed, nervousness and fatigue have been found to be the most serious reasons why applicants fail to do their best on civil service tests. Here is a list of reminders:

- Begin your preparation early – Don't wait until the last minute to go scurrying around for books and materials or to find out what the position is all about.
- Prepare continuously – An hour a night for a week is better than an all-night cram session. This has been definitely established. What is more, a night a week for a month will return better dividends than crowding your study into a shorter period of time.
- Locate the place of the exam – You have been sent a notice telling you when and where to report for the examination. If the location is in a different town or otherwise unfamiliar to you, it would be well to inquire the best route and learn something about the building.
- Relax the night before the test – Allow your mind to rest. Do not study at all that night. Plan some mild recreation or diversion; then go to bed early and get a good night's sleep.
- Get up early enough to make a leisurely trip to the place for the test – This way unforeseen events, traffic snarls, unfamiliar buildings, etc. will not upset you.
- Dress comfortably – A written test is not a fashion show. You will be known by number and not by name, so wear something comfortable.

- Leave excess paraphernalia at home – Shopping bags and odd bundles will get in your way. You need bring only the items mentioned in the official notice you received; usually everything you need is provided. Do not bring reference books to the exam. They will only confuse those last minutes and be taken away from you when in the test room.
- Arrive somewhat ahead of time – If because of transportation schedules you must get there very early, bring a newspaper or magazine to take your mind off yourself while waiting.
- Locate the examination room – When you have found the proper room, you will be directed to the seat or part of the room where you will sit. Sometimes you are given a sheet of instructions to read while you are waiting. Do not fill out any forms until you are told to do so; just read them and be prepared.
- Relax and prepare to listen to the instructions
- If you have any physical problem that may keep you from doing your best, be sure to tell the test administrator. If you are sick or in poor health, you really cannot do your best on the exam. You can come back and take the test some other time.

VII. AT THE TEST

The day of the test is here and you have the test booklet in your hand. The temptation to get going is very strong. Caution! There is more to success than knowing the right answers. You must know how to identify your papers and understand variations in the type of short-answer question used in this particular examination. Follow these suggestions for maximum results from your efforts:

1) Cooperate with the monitor

The test administrator has a duty to create a situation in which you can be as much at ease as possible. He will give instructions, tell you when to begin, check to see that you are marking your answer sheet correctly, and so on. He is not there to guard you, although he will see that your competitors do not take unfair advantage. He wants to help you do your best.

2) Listen to all instructions

Don't jump the gun! Wait until you understand all directions. In most civil service tests you get more time than you need to answer the questions. So don't be in a hurry. Read each word of instructions until you clearly understand the meaning. Study the examples, listen to all announcements and follow directions. Ask questions if you do not understand what to do.

3) Identify your papers

Civil service exams are usually identified by number only. You will be assigned a number; you must not put your name on your test papers. Be sure to copy your number correctly. Since more than one exam may be given, copy your exact examination title.

4) Plan your time

Unless you are told that a test is a "speed" or "rate of work" test, speed itself is usually not important. Time enough to answer all the questions will be provided, but this does not mean that you have all day. An overall time limit has been set. Divide the total time (in minutes) by the number of questions to determine the approximate time you have for each question.

5) Do not linger over difficult questions

If you come across a difficult question, mark it with a paper clip (useful to have along) and come back to it when you have been through the booklet. One caution if you do this – be sure to skip a number on your answer sheet as well. Check often to be sure that you have not lost your place and that you are marking in the row numbered the same as the question you are answering.

6) Read the questions

Be sure you know what the question asks! Many capable people are unsuccessful because they failed to *read* the questions correctly.

7) Answer all questions

Unless you have been instructed that a penalty will be deducted for incorrect answers, it is better to guess than to omit a question.

8) Speed tests

It is often better NOT to guess on speed tests. It has been found that on timed tests people are tempted to spend the last few seconds before time is called in marking answers at random – without even reading them – in the hope of picking up a few extra points. To discourage this practice, the instructions may warn you that your score will be "corrected" for guessing. That is, a penalty will be applied. The incorrect answers will be deducted from the correct ones, or some other penalty formula will be used.

9) Review your answers

If you finish before time is called, go back to the questions you guessed or omitted to give them further thought. Review other answers if you have time.

10) Return your test materials

If you are ready to leave before others have finished or time is called, take ALL your materials to the monitor and leave quietly. Never take any test material with you. The monitor can discover whose papers are not complete, and taking a test booklet may be grounds for disqualification.

VIII. EXAMINATION TECHNIQUES

1) Read the general instructions carefully. These are usually printed on the first page of the exam booklet. As a rule, these instructions refer to the timing of the examination; the fact that you should not start work until the signal and must stop work at a signal, etc. If there are any *special* instructions, such as a choice of questions to be answered, make sure that you note this instruction carefully.

2) When you are ready to start work on the examination, that is as soon as the signal has been given, read the instructions to each question booklet, underline any key words or phrases, such as *least, best, outline, describe* and the like. In this way you will tend to answer as requested rather than discover on reviewing your paper that you *listed without describing*, that you selected the *worst* choice rather than the *best* choice, etc.

3) If the examination is of the objective or multiple-choice type – that is, each question will also give a series of possible answers: A, B, C or D, and you are called upon to select the best answer and write the letter next to that answer on your answer paper – it is advisable to start answering each question in turn. There may be anywhere from 50 to 100 such questions in the three or four hours allotted and you can see how much time would be taken if you read through all the questions before beginning to answer any. Furthermore, if you come across a question or group of questions which you know would be difficult to answer, it would undoubtedly affect your handling of all the other questions.

4) If the examination is of the essay type and contains but a few questions, it is a moot point as to whether you should read all the questions before starting to answer any one. Of course, if you are given a choice – say five out of seven and the like – then it is essential to read all the questions so you can eliminate the two that are most difficult. If, however, you are asked to answer all the questions, there may be danger in trying to answer the easiest one first because you may find that you will spend too much time on it. The best technique is to answer the first question, then proceed to the second, etc.

5) Time your answers. Before the exam begins, write down the time it started, then add the time allowed for the examination and write down the time it must be completed, then divide the time available somewhat as follows:
   - If 3-1/2 hours are allowed, that would be 210 minutes. If you have 80 objective-type questions, that would be an average of 2-1/2 minutes per question. Allow yourself no more than 2 minutes per question, or a total of 160 minutes, which will permit about 50 minutes to review.
   - If for the time allotment of 210 minutes there are 7 essay questions to answer, that would average about 30 minutes a question. Give yourself only 25 minutes per question so that you have about 35 minutes to review.

6) The most important instruction is to *read each question* and make sure you know what is wanted. The second most important instruction is to *time yourself properly* so that you answer every question. The third most important instruction is to *answer every question.* Guess if you have to but include something for each question. Remember that you will receive no credit for a blank and will probably receive some credit if you write something in answer to an essay question. If you guess a letter – say "B" for a multiple-choice question – you may have guessed right. If you leave a blank as an answer to a multiple-choice question, the examiners may respect your feelings but it will not add a point to your score. Some exams may penalize you for wrong answers, so in such cases *only*, you may not want to guess unless you have some basis for your answer.

7) Suggestions
   a. Objective-type questions
      1. Examine the question booklet for proper sequence of pages and questions
      2. Read all instructions carefully
      3. Skip any question which seems too difficult; return to it after all other questions have been answered
      4. Apportion your time properly; do not spend too much time on any single question or group of questions

5. Note and underline key words – *all, most, fewest, least, best, worst, same, opposite,* etc.
6. Pay particular attention to negatives
7. Note unusual option, e.g., unduly long, short, complex, different or similar in content to the body of the question
8. Observe the use of "hedging" words – *probably, may, most likely,* etc.
9. Make sure that your answer is put next to the same number as the question
10. Do not second-guess unless you have good reason to believe the second answer is definitely more correct
11. Cross out original answer if you decide another answer is more accurate; do not erase until you are ready to hand your paper in
12. Answer all questions; guess unless instructed otherwise
13. Leave time for review

b. Essay questions
1. Read each question carefully
2. Determine exactly what is wanted. Underline key words or phrases.
3. Decide on outline or paragraph answer
4. Include many different points and elements unless asked to develop any one or two points or elements
5. Show impartiality by giving pros and cons unless directed to select one side only
6. Make and write down any assumptions you find necessary to answer the questions
7. Watch your English, grammar, punctuation and choice of words
8. Time your answers; don't crowd material

8) Answering the essay question

Most essay questions can be answered by framing the specific response around several key words or ideas. Here are a few such key words or ideas:

M's: manpower, materials, methods, money, management
P's: purpose, program, policy, plan, procedure, practice, problems, pitfalls, personnel, public relations

a. Six basic steps in handling problems:
1. Preliminary plan and background development
2. Collect information, data and facts
3. Analyze and interpret information, data and facts
4. Analyze and develop solutions as well as make recommendations
5. Prepare report and sell recommendations
6. Install recommendations and follow up effectiveness

b. Pitfalls to avoid
1. *Taking things for granted* – A statement of the situation does not necessarily imply that each of the elements is necessarily true; for example, a complaint may be invalid and biased so that all that can be taken for granted is that a complaint has been registered

2. *Considering only one side of a situation* – Wherever possible, indicate several alternatives and then point out the reasons you selected the best one
3. *Failing to indicate follow up* – Whenever your answer indicates action on your part, make certain that you will take proper follow-up action to see how successful your recommendations, procedures or actions turn out to be
4. *Taking too long in answering any single question* – Remember to time your answers properly

IX. AFTER THE TEST

Scoring procedures differ in detail among civil service jurisdictions although the general principles are the same. Whether the papers are hand-scored or graded by machine we have described, they are nearly always graded by number. That is, the person who marks the paper knows only the number – never the name – of the applicant. Not until all the papers have been graded will they be matched with names. If other tests, such as training and experience or oral interview ratings have been given, scores will be combined. Different parts of the examination usually have different weights. For example, the written test might count 60 percent of the final grade, and a rating of training and experience 40 percent. In many jurisdictions, veterans will have a certain number of points added to their grades.

After the final grade has been determined, the names are placed in grade order and an eligible list is established. There are various methods for resolving ties between those who get the same final grade – probably the most common is to place first the name of the person whose application was received first. Job offers are made from the eligible list in the order the names appear on it. You will be notified of your grade and your rank as soon as all these computations have been made. This will be done as rapidly as possible.

People who are found to meet the requirements in the announcement are called "eligibles." Their names are put on a list of eligible candidates. An eligible's chances of getting a job depend on how high he stands on this list and how fast agencies are filling jobs from the list.

When a job is to be filled from a list of eligibles, the agency asks for the names of people on the list of eligibles for that job. When the civil service commission receives this request, it sends to the agency the names of the three people highest on this list. Or, if the job to be filled has specialized requirements, the office sends the agency the names of the top three persons who meet these requirements from the general list.

The appointing officer makes a choice from among the three people whose names were sent to him. If the selected person accepts the appointment, the names of the others are put back on the list to be considered for future openings.

That is the rule in hiring from all kinds of eligible lists, whether they are for typist, carpenter, chemist, or something else. For every vacancy, the appointing officer has his choice of any one of the top three eligibles on the list. This explains why the person whose name is on top of the list sometimes does not get an appointment when some of the persons lower on the list do. If the appointing officer chooses the second or third eligible, the No. 1 eligible does not get a job at once, but stays on the list until he is appointed or the list is terminated.

X. HOW TO PASS THE INTERVIEW TEST

The examination for which you applied requires an oral interview test. You have already taken the written test and you are now being called for the interview test – the final part of the formal examination.

You may think that it is not possible to prepare for an interview test and that there are no procedures to follow during an interview. Our purpose is to point out some things you can do in advance that will help you and some good rules to follow and pitfalls to avoid while you are being interviewed.

What is an interview supposed to test?

The written examination is designed to test the technical knowledge and competence of the candidate; the oral is designed to evaluate intangible qualities, not readily measured otherwise, and to establish a list showing the relative fitness of each candidate – as measured against his competitors – for the position sought. Scoring is not on the basis of "right" and "wrong," but on a sliding scale of values ranging from "not passable" to "outstanding." As a matter of fact, it is possible to achieve a relatively low score without a single "incorrect" answer because of evident weakness in the qualities being measured.

Occasionally, an examination may consist entirely of an oral test – either an individual or a group oral. In such cases, information is sought concerning the technical knowledges and abilities of the candidate, since there has been no written examination for this purpose. More commonly, however, an oral test is used to supplement a written examination.

Who conducts interviews?

The composition of oral boards varies among different jurisdictions. In nearly all, a representative of the personnel department serves as chairman. One of the members of the board may be a representative of the department in which the candidate would work. In some cases, "outside experts" are used, and, frequently, a businessman or some other representative of the general public is asked to serve. Labor and management or other special groups may be represented. The aim is to secure the services of experts in the appropriate field.

However the board is composed, it is a good idea (and not at all improper or unethical) to ascertain in advance of the interview who the members are and what groups they represent. When you are introduced to them, you will have some idea of their backgrounds and interests, and at least you will not stutter and stammer over their names.

What should be done before the interview?

While knowledge about the board members is useful and takes some of the surprise element out of the interview, there is other preparation which is more substantive. It *is* possible to prepare for an oral interview – in several ways:

1) Keep a copy of your application and review it carefully before the interview

This may be the only document before the oral board, and the starting point of the interview. Know what education and experience you have listed there, and the sequence and dates of all of it. Sometimes the board will ask you to review the highlights of your experience for them; you should not have to hem and haw doing it.

2) Study the class specification and the examination announcement

Usually, the oral board has one or both of these to guide them. The qualities, characteristics or knowledges required by the position sought are stated in these documents. They offer valuable clues as to the nature of the oral interview. For example, if the job involves supervisory responsibilities, the announcement will usually indicate that knowledge of modern supervisory methods and the qualifications of the candidate as a supervisor will be tested. If so, you can expect such questions, frequently in the form of a hypothetical situation which you are expected to solve. NEVER go into an oral without knowledge of the duties and responsibilities of the job you seek.

3) Think through each qualification required

Try to visualize the kind of questions you would ask if you were a board member. How well could you answer them? Try especially to appraise your own knowledge and background in each area, *measured against the job sought*, and identify any areas in which you are weak. Be critical and realistic – do not flatter yourself.

4) Do some general reading in areas in which you feel you may be weak

For example, if the job involves supervision and your past experience has NOT, some general reading in supervisory methods and practices, particularly in the field of human relations, might be useful. Do NOT study agency procedures or detailed manuals. The oral board will be testing your understanding and capacity, not your memory.

5) Get a good night's sleep and watch your general health and mental attitude

You will want a clear head at the interview. Take care of a cold or any other minor ailment, and of course, no hangovers.

What should be done on the day of the interview?

Now comes the day of the interview itself. Give yourself plenty of time to get there. Plan to arrive somewhat ahead of the scheduled time, particularly if your appointment is in the fore part of the day. If a previous candidate fails to appear, the board might be ready for you a bit early. By early afternoon an oral board is almost invariably behind schedule if there are many candidates, and you may have to wait. Take along a book or magazine to read, or your application to review, but leave any extraneous material in the waiting room when you go in for your interview. In any event, relax and compose yourself.

The matter of dress is important. The board is forming impressions about you – from your experience, your manners, your attitude, and your appearance. Give your personal appearance careful attention. Dress your best, but not your flashiest. Choose conservative, appropriate clothing, and be sure it is immaculate. This is a business interview, and your appearance should indicate that you regard it as such. Besides, being well groomed and properly dressed will help boost your confidence.

Sooner or later, someone will call your name and escort you into the interview room. *This is it.* From here on you are on your own. It is too late for any more preparation. But remember, you asked for this opportunity to prove your fitness, and you are here because your request was granted.

What happens when you go in?

The usual sequence of events will be as follows: The clerk (who is often the board stenographer) will introduce you to the chairman of the oral board, who will introduce you to the other members of the board. Acknowledge the introductions before you sit down. Do not be surprised if you find a microphone facing you or a stenotypist sitting by. Oral interviews are usually recorded in the event of an appeal or other review.

Usually the chairman of the board will open the interview by reviewing the highlights of your education and work experience from your application – primarily for the benefit of the other members of the board, as well as to get the material into the record. Do not interrupt or comment unless there is an error or significant misinterpretation; if that is the case, do not hesitate. But do not quibble about insignificant matters. Also, he will usually ask you some question about your education, experience or your present job – partly to get you to start talking and to establish the interviewing "rapport." He may start the actual questioning, or turn it over to one of the other members. Frequently, each member undertakes the questioning on a particular area, one in which he is perhaps most competent, so you can expect each member to participate in the examination. Because time is limited, you may also expect some rather abrupt switches in the direction the questioning takes, so do not be upset by it. Normally, a board member will not pursue a single line of questioning unless he discovers a particular strength or weakness.

After each member has participated, the chairman will usually ask whether any member has any further questions, then will ask you if you have anything you wish to add. Unless you are expecting this question, it may floor you. Worse, it may start you off on an extended, extemporaneous speech. The board is not usually seeking more information. The question is principally to offer you a last opportunity to present further qualifications or to indicate that you have nothing to add. So, if you feel that a significant qualification or characteristic has been overlooked, it is proper to point it out in a sentence or so. Do not compliment the board on the thoroughness of their examination – they have been sketchy, and you know it. If you wish, merely say, "No thank you, I have nothing further to add." This is a point where you can "talk yourself out" of a good impression or fail to present an important bit of information. Remember, *you close the interview yourself.*

The chairman will then say, "That is all, Mr. _______, thank you." Do not be startled; the interview is over, and quicker than you think. Thank him, gather your belongings and take your leave. Save your sigh of relief for the other side of the door.

How to put your best foot forward

Throughout this entire process, you may feel that the board individually and collectively is trying to pierce your defenses, seek out your hidden weaknesses and embarrass and confuse you. Actually, this is not true. They are obliged to make an appraisal of your qualifications for the job you are seeking, and they want to see you in your best light. Remember, they must interview all candidates and a non-cooperative candidate may become a failure in spite of their best efforts to bring out his qualifications. Here are 15 suggestions that will help you:

1) Be natural – Keep your attitude confident, not cocky

If you are not confident that you can do the job, do not expect the board to be. Do not apologize for your weaknesses, try to bring out your strong points. The board is interested in a positive, not negative, presentation. Cockiness will antagonize any board member and make him wonder if you are covering up a weakness by a false show of strength.

2) Get comfortable, but don't lounge or sprawl

Sit erectly but not stiffly. A careless posture may lead the board to conclude that you are careless in other things, or at least that you are not impressed by the importance of the occasion. Either conclusion is natural, even if incorrect. Do not fuss with your clothing, a pencil or an ashtray. Your hands may occasionally be useful to emphasize a point; do not let them become a point of distraction.

3) Do not wisecrack or make small talk

This is a serious situation, and your attitude should show that you consider it as such. Further, the time of the board is limited – they do not want to waste it, and neither should you.

4) Do not exaggerate your experience or abilities

In the first place, from information in the application or other interviews and sources, the board may know more about you than you think. Secondly, you probably will not get away with it. An experienced board is rather adept at spotting such a situation, so do not take the chance.

5) If you know a board member, do not make a point of it, yet do not hide it

Certainly you are not fooling him, and probably not the other members of the board. Do not try to take advantage of your acquaintanceship – it will probably do you little good.

6) Do not dominate the interview

Let the board do that. They will give you the clues – do not assume that you have to do all the talking. Realize that the board has a number of questions to ask you, and do not try to take up all the interview time by showing off your extensive knowledge of the answer to the first one.

7) Be attentive

You only have 20 minutes or so, and you should keep your attention at its sharpest throughout. When a member is addressing a problem or question to you, give him your undivided attention. Address your reply principally to him, but do not exclude the other board members.

8) Do not interrupt

A board member may be stating a problem for you to analyze. He will ask you a question when the time comes. Let him state the problem, and wait for the question.

9) Make sure you understand the question

Do not try to answer until you are sure what the question is. If it is not clear, restate it in your own words or ask the board member to clarify it for you. However, do not haggle about minor elements.

10) Reply promptly but not hastily

A common entry on oral board rating sheets is "candidate responded readily," or "candidate hesitated in replies." Respond as promptly and quickly as you can, but do not jump to a hasty, ill-considered answer.

11) Do not be peremptory in your answers

A brief answer is proper – but do not fire your answer back. That is a losing game from your point of view. The board member can probably ask questions much faster than you can answer them.

12) Do not try to create the answer you think the board member wants

He is interested in what kind of mind you have and how it works – not in playing games. Furthermore, he can usually spot this practice and will actually grade you down on it.

13) Do not switch sides in your reply merely to agree with a board member

Frequently, a member will take a contrary position merely to draw you out and to see if you are willing and able to defend your point of view. Do not start a debate, yet do not surrender a good position. If a position is worth taking, it is worth defending.

14) Do not be afraid to admit an error in judgment if you are shown to be wrong

The board knows that you are forced to reply without any opportunity for careful consideration. Your answer may be demonstrably wrong. If so, admit it and get on with the interview.

15) Do not dwell at length on your present job

The opening question may relate to your present assignment. Answer the question but do not go into an extended discussion. You are being examined for a *new* job, not your present one. As a matter of fact, try to phrase ALL your answers in terms of the job for which you are being examined.

Basis of Rating

Probably you will forget most of these "do's" and "don'ts" when you walk into the oral interview room. Even remembering them all will not ensure you a passing grade. Perhaps you did not have the qualifications in the first place. But remembering them will help you to put your best foot forward, without treading on the toes of the board members.

Rumor and popular opinion to the contrary notwithstanding, an oral board wants you to make the best appearance possible. They know you are under pressure – but they also want to see how you respond to it as a guide to what your reaction would be under the pressures of the job you seek. They will be influenced by the degree of poise you display, the personal traits you show and the manner in which you respond.

ABOUT THIS BOOK

This book contains tests divided into Examination Sections. Go through each test, answering every question in the margin. We have also attached a sample answer sheet at the back of the book that can be removed and used. At the end of each test look at the answer key and check your answers. On the ones you got wrong, look at the right answer choice and learn. Do not fill in the answers first. Do not memorize the questions and answers, but understand the answer and principles involved. On your test, the questions will likely be different from the samples. Questions are changed and new ones added. If you understand these past questions you should have success with any changes that arise. Tests may consist of several types of questions. We have additional books on each subject should more study be advisable or necessary for you. Finally, the more you study, the better prepared you will be. This book is intended to be the last thing you study before you walk into the examination room. Prior study of relevant texts is also recommended. NLC publishes some of these in our Fundamental Series. Knowledge and good sense are important factors in passing your exam. Good luck also helps. So now study this Passbook, absorb the material contained within and take that knowledge into the examination. Then do your best to pass that exam.

EXAMINATION SECTION

EXAMINATION SECTION

TEST 1

DIRECTIONS: Each question or incomplete statement is followed by several suggested answers or completions. Select the one that BEST answers the question or completes the statement. *PRINT THE LETTER OF THE CORRECT ANSWER IN THE SPACE AT THE RIGHT.*

Questions 1-5.

DIRECTIONS: Questions 1 through 5 are to be answered on the basis of the extracts from Federal income tax withholding and Social Security tax tables shown below. These tables indicate the amounts which must be withheld from the employee's salary by his employer for Federal income tax and for Social Security. They are based on weekly earnings.

INCOME TAX WITHHOLDING TABLE							
The wages are		And the number of withholding allowances is					
At Least	But Less Than	5	6	7	8	9	10 or More
		The amount of income tax to be withheld shall be					
$300	$320	$24.60	$19.00	$13.80	$ 8.60	$4.00	$ 0
320	340	28.80	22.80	17.40	12.20	7.00	2.80
340	360	33.00	27.00	21.00	15.80	10.60	5.60
360	380	37.20	31.20	25.20	19.40	14.20	9.00
380	400	41.40	34.40	29.40	23.40	17.80	12.60
400	420	45.60	39.60	33.60	27.60	21.40	16.20
420	440	49.80	43.80	37.80	31.80	25.60	19.80
440	460	54.00	48.00	42.00	36.00	29.80	23.80
460	480	58.20	52.20	46.20	40.20	34.00	38.00
480	500	62.40	46.40	40.40	44.40	38.20	32.20

SOCIAL SECURITY TABLE					
WAGES			WAGES		
At Least	But Less Than	Tax to be Withheld	At Least	But Less Than	Tax to be Withheld
$333.18	$333.52	$19.50	$336.60	$336.94	$19.70
333.52	333.86	19.52	336.94	337.28	19.72
333.86	334.20	19.54	337.28	337.62	19.74
334.20	334.54	19.56	337.62	337.96	19.76
334.54	334.88	19.58	337.96	338.30	19.78
334.88	335.22	19.60	338.30	338.64	19.80
335.22	335.56	19.62	338.64	338.98	19.82
335.56	335.90	19.64	338.98	339.32	19.84
335.90	336.24	19.66	339.32	339.66	19.86
336.24	336.60	19.68	339.66	340.00	19.88

1. If an employee has a weekly wage of $379.50 and claims 6 withholding allowances, the amount of income tax to be withheld is 1.____
   A. $27.00 B. $31.20 C. $35.40 D. $37.20

2. An employee had wages of $335.60 for one week. 2.____
   With eight withholding allowances claimed, how much income tax will be withheld from his salary?
   A. $8.60 B. $12.00 C. $13.80 D. $17.40

3. How much social security tax will an employee with weekly wages of $335.60 pay? 3.____
   A. $19.60 B. $19.62 C. $19.64 D. $19.66

4. Mr. Wise earns $339.80 a week and claims seven withholding allowances. 4.____
   What is his take-home pay after income tax and social security tax are deducted?
   A. $300.32 B. $302.52 C. $319.92 D. $322.40

5. If an employee pays $19.74 in social security tax and claims eight withholding allowances, the amount of income tax that should be withheld from his wages is 5.____
   A. $8.60 B. $12.20 C. $13.80 D. $15.80

6. A fundamental rule of bookkeeping states that an individual's assets equal his liabilities plus his proprietorship (ASSETS = LIABILITIES – PROPRIETORSHIP). Which of the following statements logically follows from this rule? 6.____
   A. ASSETS = PROPRIETORSHIP – LIABILITIES
   B. LIABILITIES = ASSETS + PROPRIETORSHIP
   C. PROPRIETORSHIP = ASSETS – LIABILITIES
   D. PROPRIETORSHIP = LIABILITIES + ASSETS

7. Mr. Martin's assets consist of the following: 7.____

Cash on Hand:	$5,233.74
Furniture:	$4,925.00
Government Bonds:	$5,500.00

   What are his TOTAL assets?
   A. $10,158.74 $10,425.00 C. $10,733.74 D. $15,658.74

8. If Mr. Mitchell has $627.04 in his checking account and then writes three checks for $241.74, $13.24, and $101.97, what will be his new balance? 8.____
   A. $257.88 B. $269.08 C. $357.96 D. $368.96

9. An employee's net pay is equal to his total earnings less all deductions. 9.____
   If an employee's total earnings in a pay period are $497.05, what is his NET pay if he has the following deductions: Federal income tax, $90.32; FICA: $28.74; State tax: $18.79; City tax: $7.25; Pension: $1.88?
   A. $351.17 B. $351.07 C. $350.17 D. $350.07

10. A petty cash fund had an opening balance of $85.75 on December 1. Expenditures of $23.00, $15.65, $5.23, $14.75, and $26.38 were made out of his fund during the first 14 days of the month. Then, on December 17, another $38.50 was added to the fund.
If additional expenditures of $17.18, $3.29, and $11.64 were made during the remainder of the month, what was the FINAL balance of the petty cash fund at the end of December? 10.____
A. $6.93 B. $7.13 C. $46.51 D. $91.40

Questions 11-15.

DIRECTIONS: Questions 11 through 15 are to be answered on the basis of the following instructions.

The chart below is used by the loan division of a city retirement system for the following purposes: (1) to calculate the monthly payment a member must pay on an outstanding loan; (2) to calculate how much a member owes on an outstanding loan after he has made a number of payments.

To calculate the amount a member must pay each month in repaying his loan, look at Column II on the chart. You will notice that each entry in Column II corresponds to a number appearing under the *Months* column; for example, 1.004868 corresponds to 1 month, 0.503654 corresponds to 2 months, etc. To calculate the amount a member must pay each month, use the following procedure: multiply the amount of the load by the entry in Column II which corresponds to the number of months over which the load will be paid back. For example, if a loan of $200 is taken out for six months, multiply $200 by 0.169518, the entry in Column II which corresponds to six months.

In order to calculate the balance still owed on an outstanding loan, multiply the monthly payment by the number in Column I which corresponds to the number of monthly payments which remain to be paid on the loan. For example, if a member is supposed to pay $106.00 a month for twelve months, after seven payments, five monthly payments remain. To calculate the balance owed on the loan at this point, multiply the $106.00 monthly payment by 4.927807, the number in Column I that corresponds to five months.

Months	Column I	Column II
1	0.995156	1.004868
2	1.985491	0.503654
3	2.971029	0.336584
4	3.951793	0.253050
5	4.927807	0.202930
6	5.899092	0.169518
7	6.865673	0.145652
8	7.827572	0.127754
9	8.784811	0.113833
10	9.737414	0.102697
11	10.685402	0.093586
12	11.628798	0.085994
13	12.567624	0.079570
14	13.501902	0.074064
15	14.431655	0.069292

11. If Mr. Carson borrows $1,500 for eight months, how much will he have to pay back each month? 11.____
    A. $187.16 B. $191.63 C. $208.72 D. $218.65

12. If a member borrows $2,400 for one year, the amount he will have to pay back each month is 12.____
    A. $118.78 B. $196.18 C. $202.28 D. $206.38

13. Mr. Elliott borrowed $1,700 for a period of fifteen months. Each month he will have to pay back 13.____
    A. $117.80 B. $116.96 C. $107.79 D. $101.79

14. Mr. Aylward is paying back a thirteen-month loan at the rate of $173.13 a month. If he has already made six monthly payments, how much does he owe on the outstanding loan? 14.____
    A. $1,027.38 B. $1,178.75 C. $1,188.65 D. $1,898.85

15. A loan was taken out for 15 months, and the monthly payment was $104.75. After two monthly payments, how much was still owed on this load? 15.____
    A. $515.79 B. $863.89 C. $1,116.76 D. $1,316.46

16. The ABC Corporation had a gross income of $125,500.00 in 2015. Of this, it paid 60% for overhead. If the gross income for 2016 increased by $6,500 and the cost of overhead increased to 61% of gross income, how much more did it pay for overhead in 2016 than in 2015? 16.____
    A. $1,320 B. $5,220 C. $7,530 D. $8,052

17. After one year, Mr. Richards paid back a total of $1,695.00 as payment for a $1,500.00 loan. All the money paid over $1,500.00 was simple interest. The interest charge was MOST NEARLY 17.____
A. 13% B. 11% C. 9% D. 7%

18. A checking account has a balance of $253.36. If deposits of $36.95, $210.23, and $7.34 and withdrawals of $117.35, $23.37, and $15.98 are made, what is the NEW balance of the account? 18.____
A. $155.54 B. $351.18 C. $364.58 D. $664.58

19. In 2015, the W Realty Company spent 27% of its income on rent. If it earned $97,254.00 in 2015, the amount it paid for rent was 19.____
A. $26.258.58 B. $26,348.58 C. $27,248.58 D. $27,358.58

20. Six percent simple annual interest on $2,436.18 is MOST NEARLY 20.____
A. $145.08 B. $145.17 c. $146.08 D. $146.17

21. Assume that the XYZ Company has $10,402.72 cash on hand. If it pays $699.83 of this for rent, the amount of cash on hand would be 21.____
A. $9,792.89 B. $9,702.89 C. $9,692.89 D. $9,602.89

22. On January 31, Mr. Warren's checking account had a balance of $933.68. If he deposited $36.40 on February 2, $126.00 on February 9, and $90.02 on February 16 and wrote no checks during this period, what was the balance of his account on February 17? 22.____
A. $680.26 B. $681.26 C. $1,186.10 D. $1,187.00

23. Multiplying a number by .75 is the same as 23.____
A. multiplying it by 2/3 B. dividing it by 2/3
C. multiplying it by 3/4 D. dividing it by 3/4

24. In City Agency A, 2/3 of the employees are enrolled in a retirement system. City Agency B has the same number of employees as Agency A, and 60% of these are enrolled in a retirement system. If Agency A has a total of 660 employees, how many MORE employees does it have enrolled in a retirement system than does Agency B? 24.____
B. 36 B. 44 C. 56 D. 66

25. Net Worth is equal to Assets minus Liabilities. If, at the end of year, a textile company had assets of $98,695.83 and liabilities of $59,238.29, what was its net worth? 25.____
A. $38,478.54 B. $38,488.64 C. $39,457.54 D. $48,557.54

KEY (CORRECT ANSWERS)

1.	B	11.	B
2.	B	12.	D
3.	C	13.	A
4.	B	14.	C
5.	B	15.	D
6.	C	16.	B
7.	D	17.	A
8.	B	18.	B
9.	D	19.	A
10.	B	20.	D

21.	B
22.	C
23.	C
24.	B
25.	C

TEST 2

DIRECTIONS: Each question or incomplete statement is followed by several suggested answers or completions. Select the one that BEST answers the question or completes the statement. *PRINT THE LETTER OF THE CORRECT ANSWER IN THE SPACE AT THE RIGHT.*

Questions 1-10.

DIRECTIONS: Questions 1 through 10 below present the identification numbers, initials, and last names of employees enrolled in a city retirement system. You are to choose the option (A, B, C, or D) that has the IDENTICAL identification number, initials, and last name as those given in each question.

Sample Question

B145698 JL Jones

A. B146798 JL Jones
B. B145698 JL Jonas
C. P145698 JL Jones
D. B145698 JL Jones

The correct answer is D. Only Option D shows the identification number, initials, and last name exactly as they are in the sample question. Options A, B, and C have errors in the identification number or last name.

1. J297483 PL Robinson 1.____
   A. J294783 PL Robinson
   B. J297483 PL Robinson
   C. J297483 PI Robinson
   D. J297843 PL Robinson

2. S497662 JG Schwartz 2.____
   B. S497662 JG Schwarz
   B. S497762 JG Schwartz
   C. S497662 JG Schwartz
   D. S497663 JG Schwartz

3. G696436 LN Alberton 3.____
   A. G696436 LM Alberton
   B. G696436 LN Albertson
   C. G696346 LN Albertson
   D. G696436 LN Alberton

4. R774923 AD Aldrich 4.____
   A. R774923 AD Aldrich
   B. R744923 AD Aldrich
   C. R774932 AP Aldrich
   D. R774932 AD Allrich

5. N239638 RP Hrynyk 5.____
   A. N236938 PR Hrynyk
   B. N236938 RP Hrynyk
   C. N239638 PR Hrynyk
   D. N239638 Hrynyk

6. R156949 LT Carlson 6.____
   A. R156949 LT Carlton
   B. R156494 LT Carlson
   C. R159649 LT Carlton
   D. R156949 LT Carlson

7. T524697 MN Orenstein 7.____
   A. T524697 MN Orenstein
   B. T524967 MN Orinstein
   C. T524697 NM Ornstein
   D. T524967 NM Orenstein

8. L346239 JD Remsen 8.____
   A. L346239 JD Remson
   B. L364239 JD Remsen
   C. L346329 JD Remsen
   D. L346239 JD Remsen

9. P966438 SB Rieperson 9.____
   A. P996438 SB Rieperson
   B. P466438 SB Reiperson
   C. R996438 SB Rieperson
   D. P966438 SB Rieperson

10. D749382 CD Thompson 10.____
   A. P749382 CD Thompson
   B. D749832 CD Thomsonn
   C. D749382 CD Thompson
   D. D749823 CD Thomspon

Questions 11-20.

DIRECTIONS: Assume that each of the capital letters in the table below represents the name of an employee enrolled in the city's employees' personnel system. The number directly beneath the letter represents the agency for which the employee works, and the small letter directly beneath represents the code for the employee's account.

Name of Employee	L	O	T	Q	A	M	R	N	C
Agency	3	4	5	9	8	7	2	1	6
Account Code	r	f	b	i	d	t	g	e	n

In each of the following Questions 11 through 20, the agency code numbers and the account code letters in Columns 2 and 3 should correspond to the capital letters in Column 1 and should be in the same consecutive order. For each question, look at each column carefully and mark your answer as follows:

If there are one or more errors in Column 2 only, mark your answer A.
If there are one or more errors in Column 3 only, mark your answer B.
I there are one or more errors in Column 2 and one or more errors in Column 3, mark your answer C.
If there are NO errors in either column, mark your answer D.

Sample Question

Column 1	Column 2	Column 3
TQLMOC	583746	birtfn

In Column 2, the second agency code number (corresponding to letter Q) should be 9, not 8. Column 3 is coded correctly to Column 1. Since there is an error only in Column 2, the correct answer is A.

	COLUMN 1	COLUMN 2	COLUMN 3	
11.	QLNRCA	931268	iregnd	11.____
12.	NRMOTC	127546	egftbn	12.____
13.	RCTALM	265837	gndbrt	13.____
14.	TAMLON	578341	bdtrfe	14.____
15.	ANTORM	815427	debigt	15.____
16.	MRALON	728341	tgdrfe	16.____
17.	CTNQRO	657924	ndeigf	17.____
18.	QMROTA	972458	itgfbd	18.____
19.	RQMCOL	297463	gitnfr	19.____
20.	NOMRTQ	147259	eftgbi	20.____

Questions 21-25.

DIRECTIONS: Questions 21 through 25 are to be answered SOLELY on the basis of the following passage.

The city may issue its own bonds or it may purchase bonds as an investment. Bonds may be issued in various denominations, and the face value of the bond is its par value. Before purchasing a bond, the investor desires to know the rate of income that the investment may yield in computing the yield on a bond, it is assumed that the investor will keep the bond until the date of maturity, except for callable bonds which are not considered in this passage. To compute exact yield is a complicated mathematical problem, and scientifically prepared tables are generally used to avoid such computation. However, the approximate yield can be computed much more easily. In computing approximate yield, the accrued interest on the date of purchase should be ignored because the buyer who pays accrued interest to the seller receives it again at the next interest date. Bonds bought at a premium (which cost more) yield a lower rate of income than the same bonds bought at par (face value), and bounds bought at a discount (which cost less) yield a higher rate of income than the same bonds bought at par.

21. An investor bought a $10,000 city bond paying 6% interest. Which of the following purchase prices would indicate that the bond was bought at a premium? 21.____
    A. $9,000 B. $9,400 C. $10,000 D. $10,600

22. During 2016, a particular $10,000 bond paying 7 ½% sold at fluctuating prices. Which of the following prices would indicate that the bond was bought at a discount? 22.____
    A. $9,800 B. $10,000 C. $10,200 D. $10,750

23. A certain group of bonds was sold in denominations of$5,000, $10,000, $20,000, and $50,000. 23.____
In the following list of four purchase prices, which one is MOST likely to represent a bond sold at par value?
A. $10,500 B. $20,000 C. $22,000 D. $49,000

24. When computing the approximate yield on a bond, it is DESIRABLE to 24.____
A. assume the bond was purchased at par
B. consult scientifically prepared tables
C. ignore accrued interest on the date of purchase
D. wait until the bond reaches maturity

25. Which of the following is MOST likely to be an exception to the information provided in the above passage? 25.____
Bonds
A. purchased at a premium
B. sold at par
C. sold before maturity
D. which are callable

KEY (CORRECT ANSWERS)

1.	B	11.	D
2.	C	12.	C
3.	D	13.	B
4.	A	14.	A
5.	D	15.	B
6.	D	16.	D
7.	A	17.	C
8.	D	18.	D
9.	D	19.	A
10.	C	20.	D

21.	D
22.	A
23.	B
24.	C
25.	D

TEST 3

DIRECTIONS: Each question or incomplete statement is followed by several suggested answers or completions. Select the one that BEST answers the question or completes the statement. *PRINT THE LETTER OF THE CORRECT ANSWER IN THE SPACE AT THE RIGHT.*

Questions 1-6.

DIRECTIONS: Questions 1 through 6 consist of computations of addition, subtraction, multiplication, and division. For each question, do the computation indicated, and choose the correct answer from the four choices given.

1. ADD: 8936 1.____
   7821
   8953
   4297
   9785
   6579

   A. 45371 B. 45381 C. 46371 D. 46381

2. SUBTRACT: 95,432 2.____
   67,596

   A. 27,836 B. 27,846 C. 27,936 D. 27,946

3. MULTIPLY: 987 3.____
   867

   A. 854609 B. 854729 C. 855709 D. 855729

4. DIVIDE: 59)321439.0 4.____

   A. 5438.1 B. 5447.1 C. 5448.1 D. 5457.1

5. DIVIDE: .057)721 5.____

   A. 12,648.0 B. 12,648.1 C. 12,649.0 D. 12,649.1

6. ADD: 1/2 + 5/7 6.____
   A. 1 3/14 B. 1 2/7 C. 1 5/14 D. 1 3/7

7. If the total number of employees in one city agency increased from 1,927 to 2,006 during a certain year, the percentage increase in the number of employees for that year is MOST NEARLY 7.____
   A. 4% B. 5% C. 6% D. 7%

8. During a single fiscal year, which totaled 248 workdays, one account clerk verified 1,488 purchase vouchers. 8.____
Assuming a normal work week of five days, what is the average number of vouchers verified by the account clerk in a one-week period during this fiscal year?
A. 25 B. 30 C. 35 D. 40

9. If the city department of purchase bought 190 computers for $793.50 each and 208 computers for $839.90 each, the TOTAL price paid for these computers is 9.____
A. $315,813.00 B. $325,464.20
C. $334,279.20 D. $335,863.00

Questions 10-14.

DIRECTIONS: Questions 10 through 14 are to be answered SOLELY on the basis of the information given in the following paragraph.

Since discounts are in common use in the commercial world and apply to purchases made by government agencies as well as business firms, it is essential that individuals in both public and private employment who prepare bills, check invoices, prepare payment vouchers, or write checks to pay bills have an understanding of the terms used. These include cash or time discount, trade discount, and disconnect series. A cash or time discount offers a reduction in price to the buyer for the prompt payment of the bill and is usually expressed as a percentage with a time requirement, stated in days, within which the bill must be paid in order to earn the discount. An example would be 3/10, meaning a 3% discount may be applied to the bill if the payment is forwarded to the vendor within ten days. On an invoice, the cash discount terms are usually followed by the net terms, which is the time in days allowed for ordinary payment of the bill. Thus, 3/10, Net 30 means that full payment is expected in thirty days if the cash discount of 3% is not taken for having paid the bill within ten days. When the expression Terms Net Cash is listed on a bill, it means that no deduction for early payment is allowed. A trade discount is normally applied to list prices by a manufacturer to show the actual price to retailers so that they may know their cost and determine markups that will allow them to operate competitively and at a profit. A trade discount is applied by the seller to the list price and is independent of a cash or time discount. Discounts may also be used by manufacturers to adjust prices charged to retailers without changing list prices. This is usually done by series discounting and is expressed as a series of percentages. To compute a series discount, such as 40%, 20%, 10%, first apply the 40% discount to the list price, then apply the 20% discount to the remainder, and finally apply the 10% discount to the second remainder.

10. According to the above passage, trade discounts are 10.____
A. applied by the buyer B. independent of cash discounts
C. restricted to cash sales D. used to secure rapid payment of bills

11. According to the above passage, if the sales terms 5/10, Net 60 appear on a bill in the amount of $100 dated December 5, 2016 and the buyer submits his payment on December 15, 2016, his PROPER payment should be 11.____
A. $60 B. $90 C. $95 D. $100

12. According to the above passage, if a manufacturer gives a trade discount of 40% for an item with a list price of $250 and the terms are Net Cash, the price a retail merchant is required to pay for this item is 12.____
    A. $250 B. $210 C. $150 D. $100

13. According to the above passage, a series discount of 25%, 20%, 10% applied to a list price of $200 results in an ACTUAL price to the buyer of 13.____
    A. $88 B. $90 C. $108 D. $110

14. According to the above passage, if a manufacturer gives a trade discount of 50% and the terms are 6/10, Net 30, the cost to a retail merchant of an item with a list price of $500 and for which he takes the time discount is 14.____
    A. $220 B. $235 C. $240 D. $250

Questions 15-22.

DIRECTIONS: Questions 15 through 22 each show in Column I the information written on five cards (lettered j, k, l, m, n) which have to be filed. You are to choose the option (lettered A, B, C, or D) in Column II which BEST represents the proper order of filing according to the information, rules, and sample question given below.

A file card record is kept of the work assignments for all the employees in a certain bureau. On each card is the employee's name, the date of work assignment, and the work assignment code number. The cards are to be filed according to the following rules:

FIRST: File in alphabetical order according to employee's name.

SECOND: When two or more cards have the same employee's name, file according to the assignment date, beginning with the earliest date.

THIRD: When two or more cards have the same employee's name and the same date, file according to the work assignment number beginning with the lowest number.

Column II shows the cards arranged in four different orders. Pick the option (A, B, C, or D) in Column II which shows the correct arrangement of the cards according to th above filing rules.

SAMPLE QUESTION

Column I	Column II
j. Cluney 4/8/02 (486503)	A. k, l, m, j, n
k. Roster 5/10/01 (246611)	B. k, n, j, l, m
l. Altool 10/15/02 (711433)	C. l, k, j, m, n
m. Cluney 12/18/02 (527610)	D. l, n, j, m, k
n. Cluney 4/8/02 (486500)	

The correct way to file the cards is:

l. Altool 10/15/02 (71143)
n. Cluney 4/8/02 (486500)
j. Cluney 4/8/02 (486503)
m. Cluney 12/18/02 (527610)
k. Roster 5/10/01 (246611)

The correct filing order is shown by the letters l, n, j, m, k. The answer to the sample question is the letter D, which appears in front of the letters l, n, j, m, k in Column II.

	COLUMN I	COLUMN II	
15.	j. Smith 3/19/03 (662118)	A. j, m, l, n, k	15.____
	k. Turner 4/16/99 (481349)	B. j, l, n, m, k	
	l. Terman 3/20/02 (210229)	C. k, n, m, l, j	
	m. Smyth 3/20/02 (481359)	D. j, n, k, l, m	
	n. Terry 5/11/01 (672128)		
16.	j. Ross 5/29/02 (396118)	A. l, m, k, n, j	16.____
	k. Rosner 5/29/02 (439281)	B. m, l, k, n, j	
	l. Rose 7/19/02 (723456)	C. l, m, k, j, n	
	m. Rosen 5/29/03 (829692)	D. m, l, j, n, k	
	n. Ross 5/29/02 (399118)		
17.	j. Sherd 10/12/99 (552368)	A. n, m, k, j, l	17.____
	k. Snyder 11/12/99 (539286)	B. j, m, l, k, n	
	l. Shindler 10/13/98 (426798)	C. m, k, n, j. l	
	m. Scherld 10/12/99 (552386)	D. m, n, j, l, k	
	n. Schneider 11/12/99 (798213)		
18.	j. Carter 1/16/02 (489636)	A. k, n, j, l, m	18.____
	k. Carson 2/16/01 (392671)	B. n, k, m, l, j	
	l. Carter 1/16/01 (486936)	C. n, k, l, j, m	
	m. Carton 3/15/00 (489639)	D. k, n, l, j, m	
	n. Carson 2/16/01 (392617)		
19.	j. Thomas 3/18/99 (763182)	A. m, l, j, k, n	19.____
	k. Tompkins 3/19/00 (928439)	B. j, m, l, k, n	
	l. Thomson 3/21/00 (763812)	C. j, l, n, m, k	
	m. Thompson 3/18/99 (924893)	D. l, m, j, n, k	
	n. Tompson 3/19/99 (928793)		
20.	j. Breit 8/10/03 (345612)	A. m, j, n, k, l	20.____
	k. Briet 5/21/00 (837543)	B. n, m, j, k, l	
	l. Bright 9/18/99 (931827)	C. m, j, k, l, n	
	m. Breit 3/7/98 (553984)	D. j, m, k, l, n	
	n. Brent 6/14/04 (682731)		

COLUMN I	COLUMN II	
21. j. Roberts 10/19/02 (581932) k. Rogers 8/9/00 (638763) l. Rogerts 7/15/97 (105689) m. Robin 3/8/92 (287915) n. Rogers 4/2/04 (736921)	A. n, k, l, m, j B. n, k, l, j, m C. k, n, l, m, j D. j, m, k, n, l	21.____
22. j. Hebert 4/28/02 (719468) k. Herbert 5/8/01 (938432) l. Helbert 9/23/04 (832912) m. Herbst 7/10/03 (648599) n. Herbert 5/8/01 (487627)	A. n, k, j, m, l B. j, l, n, k, m C. l, j, k, n, m D. l, j, n, k, m	22.____

23. In order to pay its employees, the Convex Company obtained bills and coins in the following denominations: 23.____

Denomination	$20	$10	$5	$1	$.50	$.25	$.10	$.05	$.01
Number	317	122	38	73	69	47	39	25	36

What was the TOTAL amount of cash obtained?
A. $7,874.76 B. $7,878.00 C. $7,889.25 D. $7,924.35

24. H. Partridge receives a weekly gross salary (before deductions) of $596.25. Through weekly payroll deductions of $19.77, he is paying back a load he took from his pension fund. 24.____
If other fixed weekly deductions amount to $184.14, how much pay would Mr. Partridge take home over a period of 33 weeks?
A. $11,446.92 B. $12,375.69 C. $12,947.22 D. $19,676.25

25. Mr. Robertson is a city employee enrolled in a city retirement system. He has taken out a loan from the retirement fund and is paying it back at the rate of $14.90 every two weeks. 25.____
In eighteen weeks, how much money will he have paid back on the loan?
A. $268.20 B. $152.80 C. $124.10 D. $67.05

26. In 2015, the Iridor Book Company had the following expenses: rent, $6,500; overhead, $52,585; inventory, $35,700; and miscellaneous, $1,275. 26.____
If all of these expenses went up 18% in 2016, what would they TOTAL in 2016?
A. $17,290.80 B. $78,768.20 C. $96,060.00 D. $113,350.80

27. Ms. Ranier had a gross salary of $355.36, paid once every week. 27.____
If the deductions from each paycheck are $62.72, $25.13, $6.29, and $1,27, how much money would Ms. Ranier take home in four weeks?
A. $1,039.80 B. $1,421.44 C. $2,079.60 D. $2,842.88

28. Mr. Martin had a net income of $19,100 for the year. 28.____
If he spent 34% on rent and household expenses, 3% on house furnishings, 25% on clothes, and 36% on food, how much was left for savings and other expenses?
A. $196.00 B. $382.00 C. $649.40 D. $1,960.00

29. Mr. Elsberg can pay back a loan of $1,800 from the city employees' retirement system if he pays back $36.69 every two weeks for two full years. 29.____
At the end of the two years, how much more than the original $1,800 he borrowed will Mr. Elsberg have paid back?
A. $53.94 B. $107.88 C. $190.79 D. $214.76

30. Mrs. Nusbaum is a city employee, receiving a gross salary (salary before deductions) of $31,200. Every two weeks, the following deductions are taken out of her salary: Federal Income Tax, $243.96; FICA, $66.39; State Tax, $44.58; City Tax, $20.91; Health Insurance, $4.71. 30.____
If Mrs. Nusbaum's salary and deductions remained the same for a full calendar year, what would her NET salary (gross salary less deductions) be in that year?
A. $9,894.30 B. $21,305.70 C. $28,118.25 D. $30,819.45

KEY (CORRECT ANSWERS)

1.	C	11.	C	21.	D
2.	A	12.	C	22.	B
3.	D	13.	C	33.	A
4.	C	14.	B	24.	C
5.	D	15.	A	25.	C
6.	A	16.	C	26.	D
7.	A	17.	D	27.	A
8.	B	18.	C	28.	B
9.	B	19.	B	29.	B
10.	B	20.	A	30.	B

EXAMINATION SECTION

TEST 1

DIRECTIONS: Each question or incomplete statement is followed by several suggested answers or completions. Select the one that BEST answers the question or completes the statement. *PRINT THE LETTER OF THE CORRECT ANSWER IN THE SPACE AT THE RIGHT.*

Questions 1-4.

DIRECTIONS: Questions 1 through 4 are to be answered SOLELY on the basis of the following passage.

Job analysis combined with performance appraisal is an excellent method of determining training needs of individuals. The steps in this method are to determine the specific duties of the job, to evaluate the adequacy with which the employee performs each of these duties, and finally to determine what significant improvements can be made by training.

The list of duties can be obtained in a number of ways: asking the employee, asking the supervisor, observing the employee, etc. Adequacy of performance can be estimated by the employee, but the supervisor's evaluation must also be obtained. This evaluation will usually be based on observation.

What does the supervisor observe? The employee, while he is working; the employee's work relationships; the ease, speed, and sureness of the employee's actions; the way he applies himself to the job; the accuracy and amount of completed work; its conformity with established procedures and standards; the appearance of the work; the soundness of judgment it shows; and, finally, signs of good or poor communication, understanding, and cooperation among employees.

Such observation is a normal and inseparable part of the everyday job of supervision. Systematically, recorded, evaluated, and summarized, it highlights both general and individual training needs.

1. According to the passage, job analysis may be used by the supervisor in 1.____
   A. increasing his own understanding of tasks performed in his unit
   B. increasing efficiency of communication within the organization
   C. assisting personnel experts in the classification of positions
   D. determining in which areas an employee needs more instruction

2. According to the passage, the FIRST step in determining the training needs of employees is to 2.____
   A. locate the significant improvements that can be made by training
   B. determine the specific duties required in a job
   C. evaluate the employee's performance
   D. motivate the employee to want to improve himself

3. On the basis of the above passage, which of the following is the BEST way for a supervisor to determine the adequacy of employee performance? 3.____
   A. Check the accuracy and amount of completed work
   B. Ask the training officer
   C. Observe all aspects of the employee's work
   D. Obtain the employee's own estimate

4. Which of the following is NOT mentioned by the passage as a factor to be taken into consideration in judging the adequacy of employee performance? 4.____
   A. Accuracy of completed work
   B. Appearance of completed work
   C. Cooperation among employees
   D. Attitude of the employee toward his supervisor

5. In indexing names of business firms and other organizations, ONE of the rules to be followed is: 5.____
   A. The word *and* is considered an indexing unit.
   B. When a firm name includes the full name of a person who is not well-known, the person's first name is considered as the first indexing unit.
   C. Usually the units in a firm name are indexed in the order in which they are written.
   D. When a firm's name is made up of single letters (such as ABC Corp.), the letters taken together are considered more than one indexing unit.

6. Assume that people often come to your office with complaints of errors in your agency's handling of their clients. The employees in your office have the job of listening to these complaints and investigating them. One day, when it is almost closing time, a person comes into your office, apparently very angry, and demands that you take care of his complaint at once. 6.____
   Your IMMEDIATE reaction should be to
   A. suggest that he return the following day
   B. find out his name and the nature of his complaint
   C. tell him to write a letter
   D. call over your supervisor

7. Assume that part of your job is to notify people concerning whether their applications for a certain program have been approved or disapproved. However, you do not actually make the decision on approval or disapproval. One day, you answer a telephone call from a woman who states that she has not yet received any word on her application. She goes on to tell you her qualifications for the program. From what she has said, you know that persons with such qualifications are usually approved. 7.____
   Of the following, which one is the BEST thing for you to say to her?
   A. "You probably will be accepted, but wait until you receive a letter before trying to join the program."
   B. "Since you seem well qualified, I am sure that your application will be approved."

C. "If you can write us a letter emphasizing your qualifications, it may speed up the process."
D. "You will be notified of the results of your application as soon as a decision has been made."

8. Suppose that one of your duties includes answering specific telephone inquiries. Your superior refers a call to you from an irate person who claims that your agency is inefficient and is wasting taxpayers' money. 8.____
Of the following, the BEST way to handle such a call is to
A. listen briefly and then hang up without answering
B. note the caller's comments and tell him that you will transmit them to your superiors
C. connect the caller with the head of your agency
D. discuss your own opinions with the caller

9. An employee has been assigned to open her division head's mail and place it on his desk. One day, the employee opens a letter which she then notices is marked *Personal*. 9.____
Of the following, the BEST action for her to take is to
A. write *Personal* on the letter and staple the envelope to the back of the letter
B. ignore the matter and treat the letter the same way as the others
C. give it to another division head to hold until her own division head comes into the office
D. leave the letter in the envelope and write *Sorry opened by mistake* on the envelope and initial it

Questions 10-14.

DIRECTIONS: Questions 10 through 14 each consist of a quotation which contains one word that is incorrectly used because it is not in keeping with the meaning that the quotation is evidently intended to convey. Of the words underlined in each quotation, determine which word is incorrectly used. Then select from among the words lettered A, B, C, and D the word which, when substituted for the incorrectly used word, would BEST help to convey the meaning of the quotation. (Do not indicate a change for an underlined word unless the underlined word is incorrectly used.)

10. Unless reasonable managerial supervision is <u>exercised</u> over office supplies, it is certain that there will be extravagance, <u>rejected</u> items out of stock, <u>excessive</u> prices paid for certain items, and <u>obsolete</u> material in the stockroom. 10.____
A. overlooked B. immoderate C. needed D. instituted

11. Since <u>office</u> supplies are in such <u>common</u> use, an attitude of indifference about their handling is not <u>unusual</u>. Their importance is often recognized only when they are <u>utilized</u> or out of stock, for office employees must have proper supplies if maximum productivity is to be <u>attained</u>. 11.____
A. plentiful B. unavailable C. reduced D. expected

12. Anyone <u>effected</u> by paperwork, <u>interested</u> in or engaged in office work, or desiring to improve <u>informational</u> activities can find materials <u>keyed</u> to his needs. 12.____
    A. attentive B. available C. affected D. ambitious

13. Information is <u>homogeneous</u> and must therefore be properly classified so that each type may be <u>employed</u> in ways <u>appropriate</u> to its <u>own peculiar</u> properties. 13.____
    A. apparent
    B. heterogeneous
    C. consistent
    D. idiosyncratic

14. <u>Intellectual</u> training may seem a <u>formidable</u> phrase, but it means nothing more than the <u>deliberate</u> cultivation of the ability to think, and there is no <u>dark</u> contrast between the intellectual and the practical. 14.____
    A. subjective B. objective C. sharp D. vocational

15. The MOST important reason for having a filing system is to 15.____
    A. get papers out of the way
    B. have a record of everything that has happened
    C. retain information to justify your actions
    D. enable rapid retrieval of information

16. The system of filing which is used MOST frequently is called _____ filing. 16.____
    A. alphabetic
    B. alphanumeric
    C. geographic
    D. numeric

17. One of the clerks under your supervision has been telephoning frequently to tell you that he was taking the day off. Unless there is a real need for it, taking leave which is not scheduled is frowned upon because it upsets the work schedule. 17.____
    Under these circumstances, which of the following reasons for taking the day off is MOST acceptable?
    A. "I can't work when my arthritis bothers me."
    B. "I've been pressured with work from my night job and needed the extra time to catch up."
    C. "My family just moved to a new house, and I needed the time to start the repairs."
    D. "Work here has not been challenging, and I've been looking for another job."

18. One of the employees under your supervision, previously a very satisfactory worker, has begun arriving late one or two mornings each week. No explanation has been offered for this change. You call her to your office for a conference. As you are explaining the purpose of the conference and your need to understand this sudden lateness problem, she becomes very angry and states that you have no right to question her. 18.____
    Of the following, the BEST course of action for you to take at this point is to

A. inform her in your most authoritarian tone that you are the supervisor and that you have every right to question her
B. end the conference and advise the employee that you will have no further discussion with her until she controls her temper
C. remain calm, try to calm her down, and when she has quieted, explain the reasons for your questions and the need for answers
D. hold your temper; when she has calmed down, tell her that you will not have a tardy worker in your unit and will have her transferred at once

19. Assume that, in the branch of the agency for which you work, you are the only clerical person on the staff with a supervisory title and, in addition, that you are the office manager. On a particular day when all members of the professional staff are away from the building attending an important meeting, an urgent call comes through requesting some confidential information ordinarily released only by professional staff. 19.____
Of the following, the MOST reasonable action for you to take is to
A. decline to give the information because you are not a member of the professional staff
B. offer to call back after you get permission from the agency director at the main office
C. advise the caller that you will supply the information as soon as your chief returns
D. supply the information requested and inform your chief when she returns

20. As a supervisor, you are scheduled to attend an important conference with your superior. However, that day you learn that your very capable assistant is ill and unable to come to work. Several highly sensitive tasks are scheduled for completion on this day. 20.____
Of the following, the BEST way to handle this situation is to
A. tell your supervisor you cannot attend the meeting and ask that it be postponed
B. assign one of your staff to see that the jobs are completed and turned in
C. advise your supervisor of the situation and ask what you should do
D. call the departments for which the work is being done and ask for an extension of time

21. When a decision needs to be made which is likely to affect units other than his own, a supervisor should USUALLY 21.____
A. make such a decision quickly and then discuss it with his supervisor
B. make such a decision only after careful consultation with his subordinates
C. discuss the problem with his immediate superior before making such a decision
D. have his subordinates arrive at such a decision in conference with the subordinates in the other units

22. Assume that, as a supervisor in Division X, you are training Ms. Y, a new employee, to answer the telephone properly. 22.____
You should explain that the BEST way to answer is to pick up the receiver and say:

A. "What is your name, please?"
B. "May I help you?"
C. "Ms. Y speaking."
D. "Division X, Ms. Y speaking."

Questions 23-25.

DIRECTIONS: Questions 23 through 25 consist of sentences in which two words are missing. Examine each sentence, and then choose from below it the words which should be inserted in the blank spaces in order to create a coherent and well-written sentence.

23. Human behavior is far _____ variable, and therefore _____ predictable, than that of any other species. 23.____
A. less; as
B. less; not
C. more; not
D. more; less

24. The _____ limitation of this method is that the results are based _____ a narrow sample. 24.____
A. chief; with
B. chief; on
C. only; for
D. only; to

25. Although there _____ a standard procedure for handling these problems, each case often has _____ own unique features. 25.____
A. are; its
B. are; their
C. is; its
D. is; their

KEY (CORRECT ANSWERS)

1.	D	11.	B
2.	B	12.	C
3.	C	13.	B
4.	D	14.	C
5.	C	15.	D
6.	B	16.	A
7.	D	17.	A
8.	B	18.	C
9.	D	19.	B
10.	C	20.	C

21.	C
22.	D
23.	D
24.	B
25.	C

TEST 2

DIRECTIONS: Each question or incomplete statement is followed by several suggested answers or completions. Select the one that BEST answers the question or completes the statement. *PRINT THE LETTER OF THE CORRECT ANSWER IN THE SPACE AT THE RIGHT.*

Questions 1-3.

DIRECTIONS: Questions 1 through 3 each consist of a group of four sentences. Read each sentence carefully, and select the one of the four in each group which represents the BEST English usage for business letters and reports.

1. A. The chairman himself, rather than his aides, has reviewed the report. 1.____
   B. The chairman himself, rather than his aides, have reviewed the report.
   C. The chairmen, not the aide, has reviewed the report.
   D. The aide, not the chairmen, have reviewed the report.

2. A. Various proposals were submitted but the decision is not been made. 2.____
   B. Various proposals has been submitted but the decision has not been made.
   C. Various proposals were submitted but the decision is not been made.
   D. Various proposals have been submitted but the decision has not been made.

3. A. Everyone were rewarded for his successful attempt. 3.____
   B. They were successful in their attempts and each of them was rewarded.
   C. Each of them are rewarded for their successful attempts.
   D. The reward for their successful attempts were made to each of them.

4. Which of the following is MOST suited to arrangement in chronological order? 4.____
   A. Applications for various types and levels of jobs
   B. Issues of a weekly publication
   C. Weekly time cards for all employees for the week of April 21
   D. Personnel records for all employees

5. Words that are *synonymous* with a given word ALWAYS _____ the given word. 5.____
   A. have the same meaning as
   B. have the same pronunciation as
   C. have the opposite meaning of
   D. can be rhymed with

Questions 6-11.

DIRECTIONS: Questions 6 through 11 are to be answered on the basis of the following chart showing numbers of errors made by four clerks in one work unit for a half-year period.

	Allan	Barry	Cary	David
July	5	4	1	7
August	8	3	9	8
September	7	8	7	5
October	3	6	5	3
November	2	4	4	6
December	5	2	8	4

6. The clerk with the HIGHEST number of errors for the six-month period was 6.____
   A. Allan B. Barry C. Cary D. David

7. If the number of errors made by Allan in the six months shown represented one-eighth of the total errors made by the unit during the entire year, what was the TOTAL number of errors made by the unit for the year? 7.____
   A. 124 B. 180 C. 240 D. 360

8. The number of errors made by David in November was what FRACTION of the total errors made in November? 8.____
   A. 1/3 B. 1/6 C. 3/8 D. 3/16

9. The average number of errors made per month per clerk was MOST NEARLY 9.____
   A. 4 B. 5 C. 6 D. 7

10. Of the total number of errors made during the six-month period, the percentage made in August was MOST NEARLY 10.____
    A. 2% B. 4% C. 23% D. 4%

11. If the number of errors in the unit were to decrease in the next six months by 30%, what would be MOST NEARLY the total number of errors for the unit for the next six months? 11.____
    A. 87 B. 94 C. 120 D. 137

12. The arithmetic mean salary for five employees earning $18,500, $18,300, $18,600, $18,400, and $18,500, respectively is 12.____
    A. $18,450 B. $18,460 C. $18,475 D. $18,500

13. Last year, a city department which is responsible for purchasing supplies ordered bond paper in equal quantities from 22 different companies. The price was exactly the same for each company, and the total cost for the 22 orders was $693,113. 13.____
    Assuming prices did not change during the year, the cost of EACH order was MOST NEARLY
    A. $31,490 B. $31,495 C. $31,500 D. $31,505

14. A city agency engaged in repair work uses a small part which the city purchases for $0.14 each. Assume that, in a certain year, the total expenditure of the city for this part was $700.
How MANY of these parts were purchased that year? 14.____
A. 50 B. 200 C. 2,000 D. 5,000

15. The work unit which you supervise is responsible for processing fifteen reports per month.
If your unit has four clerks and the best worker completes 40% of the reports himself, how many reports would each of the other clerks have to complete if they all do an equal number? 15.____
A. 1 B. 2 C. 3 D. 4

16. Assume that the work unit in which you work has 24 clerks and 18 stenographers. In order to change the ratio of stenographers to clerks so that there is one stenographer for every four clerks, it would be necessary to REDUCE the number of stenographers by 16.____
A. 3 B. 6 C. 9 D. 12

17. Assume that your office is responsible for opening and distributing all the mail of the division. After opening a letter, one of your subordinates notices that it states that there should be an enclosure in the envelope. However, there is no enclosure in the envelope.
Of the following, the BEST instruction that you can give the clerk is to 17.____
A. call the sender to obtain the enclosure
B. call the addressee to inform him that the enclosure is missing
C. note the omission in the margin of the letter
D. forward the letter without taking any action

18. While opening the envelope containing official correspondence, you accidentally cut the enclosed letter.
Of the following, the BEST action for you to take is to 18.____
A. leave the material as it is
B. put it together by using transparent mending tape
C. keep it together by putting it back in the envelope
D. keep it together by using paper clips

19. Suppose your supervisor is on the telephone in his office and an applicant arrives for a scheduled interview with him.
Of the following, the BEST procedure to follow ordinarily is to 19.____
A. informally chat with the applicant in your office until your supervisor has finished his phone conversation
B. escort him directly into your supervisor's office and have him wait for him there
C. inform your supervisor of the applicant's arrival and try to make the applicant feel comfortable while waiting
D. have him hang up his coat and tell him to go directly in to see your supervisor

20. The length of time that files should be kept is GENERALLY 20.____
    A. considered to be seven years
    B. dependent upon how much new material has accumulated in the files
    C. directly proportionate to the number of years the office has been in operation
    D. dependent upon the type and nature of the material in the files

21. Cross-referencing a document when you file it means 21.____
    A. making a copy of the document and putting the copy into a related file
    B. indicating on the front of the document the name of the person who wrote it, the date it was written, and for what purpose
    C. putting a special sheet or card in a related file to indicate where the document is filed
    D. indicating on the document where it is to be filed

22. Unnecessary handling and recording of incoming mail could be eliminated by 22.____
    A. having the person who opens it initial it
    B. indicating on the piece of mail the names of all the individuals who should see it
    C. sending all incoming mail to more than one central location
    D. making a photocopy of each piece of incoming mail

23. Of the following, the office tasks which lend themselves MOST readily to planning and study are 23.____
    A. repetitive, occur in volume, and extend over a period of time
    B. cyclical in nature, have small volume, and extend over a short period of time
    C. tasks which occur only once in a great while not according to any schedule, and have large volume
    D. special tasks which occur only once, regardless of their volume and length of time

24. A good recordkeeping system includes all of the following procedures EXCEPT the 24.____
    A. filing of useless records
    B. destruction of certain files
    C. transferring of records from one type of file to another
    D. creation of inactive files

25. Assume that, as a supervisor, you are responsible for orienting and training new employees in your unit. 25.____
    Which of the following can MOST properly be omitted from your discussions with a new employee?
    A. The purpose of commonly used office forms
    B. Time and leave regulations
    C. Procedures for required handling of routine business calls
    D. The reason the last employee was fired

KEY (CORRECT ANSWERS)

1.	A	11.	A
2.	D	12.	B
3.	B	13.	D
4.	B	14.	D
5.	A	15.	C
6.	C	16.	D
7.	C	17.	C
8.	C	18.	B
9.	B	19.	C
10.	C	20.	D

21.	C
22.	B
23.	A
24.	A
25.	D

SUPERVISION, ADMINISTRATION, MANAGEMENT AND ORGANIZATION
EXAMINATION SECTION

TEST 1

DIRECTIONS: Each question or incomplete statement is followed by several suggested answers or completions. Select the one that BEST answers the question or completes the statement. *PRINT THE LETTER OF THE CORRECT ANSWER IN THE SPACE AT THE RIGHT.*

1. The one of the following situations in which you as a supervisor of a group of clerks would probably be able to function MOST effectively from the viewpoint of departmental efficiency is where you are responsible DIRECTLY to 1.____
   A. a single supervisor having sole jurisdiction over you
   B. two or three supervisors having coordinate jurisdiction over you
   C. four or five supervisors having coordinate jurisdiction over you
   D. all individuals of higher rank than you in the department

2. Suppose that it is necessary to order one of the clerks under your supervision to stay overtime a few hours one evening. The work to be done is not especially difficult. It is the custom in your office to make such assignments by rotation. The particular clerk whose turn it is to work overtime requests to be excused that evening, but offers to work the next time that overtime is necessary. Hitherto, this clerk has always been very cooperative. 2.____
   Of the following, the BEST action for you to take is to
   A. grant the clerk's request, but require her to work overtime two additional nights to compensate for this concession
   B. inform the clerk that you are compelled to refuse any request for special consideration
   C. grant the clerk's request if another clerk is willing to substitute for her
   D. refuse the clerk's request outright because granting her request may encourage her to evade other responsibilities

3. When asked to comment upon the efficiency of Miss Jones, a clerk, her supervisor said, "Since she rarely makes an error, I consider her very efficient." 3.____
   Of the following, the MOST valid assumption underlying this supervisor's comment is that
   A. speed and accuracy should be considered separately in evaluating a clerk's efficiency
   B. the most accurate clerks are not necessarily the most efficient
   C. accuracy and competency are directly related
   D. accuracy is largely dependent upon the intelligence of a clerk

4. The one of the following which is the MOST accurate statement of one of the functions of a supervisor is to 4.____
   A. select scientifically the person best fitted for the specific job to be done
   B. train the clerks assigned to you in the best methods of doing the work of your office
   C. fit the job to be done to the clerks who are available
   D. assign a clerk only to those tasks for which she has the necessary experience

5. Assume that you, an experienced supervisor, are given a newly appointed clerk to assist you in performing a certain task. The new clerk presents a method of doing the task which is different from your method but which is obviously better and easy to adopt. 5.____
   Of the following you, the supervisor, should
   A. take the suggestion and try it out, even though it was offered by someone less experienced
   B. reject the idea, even though it appears an improvement, as it very likely would not work out
   C. send the new clerk away and get someone else to assist who will be more in accord with your ideas
   D. report him to the head of the office and ask that the new clerk be instructed to do things your way

6. As a supervisor, you should realize that the one of the following general abilities of a junior clerk which is probably LEAST susceptible to improvement by practice and training is 6.____
   A. intelligence
   B. speed of typing
   C. knowledge of office procedures
   D. accuracy of filing

7. As a supervisor, when training an employee, you should NOT 7.____
   A. correct errors as he makes them
   B. give him too much material to absorb at one time
   C. have him try the operation until he can do it perfectly
   D. treat any foolish question seriously

8. If a supervisor cannot check readily all the work in her unit, she should 8.____
   A. hold up the work until she can personally check it
   B. refuse to take additional work
   C. work overtime until she can personally finish it
   D. delegate part of the work to a qualified subordinate

9. The one of the following over which a unit supervisor has the LEAST control is 9.____
   A. the quality of the work done in his unit
   B. the nature of the work handled in his unit
   C. the morale of workers in his unit
   D. increasing efficiency of his unit

10. Suppose that you have received a note from an important official in your department commending the work of a unit of clerks under your supervision. Of the following, the BEST action for you to take is to 10.____
   A. withhold the note for possible use at a time when the morale of the unit appears to be declining
   B. show the note only to the better members of your staff as a reward for their good work
   C. show the note only to the poorer members of your staff as a stimulus for better work
   D. post the note conspicuously so that it can be seen by all members of your staff

11. If you find that one of your subordinates is becoming apathetic towards his work, you should 11.____
   A. prefer charges against him
   B. change the type of work
   C. request his transfer
   D. advise him to take a medical examination to check his health

12. Suppose that a new clerk has been assigned to the unit which you supervise. To give this clerk a brief picture of the functioning of your unit in the entire department would be 12.____
   A. *commendable*, because she will probably be able to perform her work with more understanding
   B. *undesirable*, because such action will probably serve only to confuse her
   C. *commendable*, because, if transferred, she would probably be able to work efficiently without additional training
   D. *undesirable*, because in-service training has been demonstrated to be less efficient than on-the-job training

13. Written instructions to a subordinate are of value because they 13.____
   A. can be kept up-to-date
   B. encourage initiative
   C. make a job seem easier
   D. are an aid in training

14. Suppose that you have assigned a task to a clerk under your supervision and have given appropriate instructions. After a reasonable period, you check her work and find that one specific aspect of her work is consistently incorrect. Of the following, the BEST action for you to take is to 14.____
   A. determine whether the clerk has correctly understood instructions concerning the aspect of the work not being done correctly
   B. assign the task to a more competent clerk
   C. wait for the clerk to commit a more flagrant error before taking up the matter with her
   D. indicate to the clerk that you are dissatisfied with her work and wait to see whether she is sufficiently intelligent to correct her own mistakes

15. If you wanted to check on the accuracy of the filing in your unit, you would 15.____
A. check all the files thoroughly at regular intervals
B. watch the clerks while they are filing
C. glance through filed papers at random
D. inspect thoroughly a small section of the files selected at random

16. In making job assignments to his subordinates, a supervisor should follow the principle that each individual generally is capable of 16.____
A. performing one type of work well and less capable of performing other types well
B. learning to perform a wide variety of different types of work
C. performing best the type of work in which he has had least experience
D. learning to perform any type of work in which he is given training

17. Of the following, the information that is generally considered MOST essential in a departmental organization survey chart is the 17.____
A. detailed operations of the department
B. lines of authority
C. relations of the department to other departments
D. names of the employees of the department

18. Suppose you are the supervisor in charge of a large unit in which all of the clerical staff perform similar tasks. 18.____
In evaluating the relative accuracy of the clerks, the clerk who should be considered to be the LEAST accurate is the one
A. whose errors result in the greatest financial loss
B. whose errors cost the most to locate
C. who makes the greatest percentage of errors in his work
D. who makes the greatest number of errors in the unit

19. Aside from requirements imposed by authority, the frequency with which reports are submitted or the length of the interval which they cover should depend PRINCIPALLY on the 19.____
A. availability of the data to be included in the reports
B. amount of time required to prepare the reports
C. extent of the variations in the data with the passage of time
D. degree of comprehensiveness required in the reports

20. A serious error has been discovered by a critical superior in work carried on under your supervision. 20.____
It is BEST to explain the situation and prevent its recurrence by
A. claiming that you are not responsible because you do not check the work personally
B. accepting the complaint and reporting the name of the employee responsible for the error
C. assuring him that you hope it will not occur again
D. assuring him that you will find out how it occurred, so that you can have the work checked with greater care in the future

21. A serious procedural problem develops in your office. 21.____
In your solution of this problem, the very FIRST step to take is to
   A. select the personnel to help you
   B. analyze your problem
   C. devise the one best method of research
   D. develop an outline of your report

22. Your office staff consists of eight clerks, stenographers, and typists, cramped in a long narrow room. The room is very difficult to ventilate properly, and, as in so many other offices, the disagreement over the method of ventilation is marked. Two cliques are developing and the friction is carrying over into the work of the office. 22.____
Of the following, the BEST way to proceed is to
   A. call your staff together, have the matter fully discussed giving each person an opportunity to be heard, and put the matter to a vote; then enforce the method of ventilation which has the most votes
   B. call your staff together and have the matter fully discussed. If a compromise arrangement is agreed upon, put it into effect. Otherwise, on the basis of all the facts at your disposal, make a decision as to how best to ventilate the room and enforce your decision
   C. speak to the employees individually, make a decision as to how to ventilate the room, and then enforce your decision
   D. study the layout of the office, make a decision as to how best to ventilate the room, and then enforce your decision

23. An organization consisting of six levels of authority, where eight persons are assigned to each supervisor on each level, would consist of APPROXIMATELY _____ persons. 23.____
   A. 50   B. 500   C. 5,000   D. 50,000

24. The one of the following which is considered by political scientists to be a GOOD principle of municipal government is 24.____
   A. concentration of authority and responsibility
   B. the long ballot
   C. low salaries and a narrow range in salaries
   D. short terms for elected city officials

25. Of the following, the statement concerning the organization of a department which is TRUE is: 25.____
   A. In general, no one employee should have active and constant supervision over more than ten persons.
   B. It is basically unwise to have a supervisor with only three subordinates.
   C. It is desirable that there be no personal contact between the rank and file employee and the supervisor once removed from him.
   D. There should be no more than four levels of authority between the top administrative office in a department and the rank and file employees.

26. Assuming that Dictaphones are not available, of the following, the situation in which it would be MOST desirable to establish a central stenographic unit is one in which the unit would serve 26.____
    A. ten correspondence clerks assigned to full-time positions answering correspondence of a large government department
    B. seven members of a government commission heading a large department
    C. seven heads of bureaus in a government department consisting of 250 employees
    D. fifty investigators in a large department

27. You are assigned to review the procedures in an office in order to recommend improvements to the commissioner directly. You go into an office performing seen routine operations in the processing of one type of office form. 27.____
    The question you should FIRST ask yourself in your study of any one of these operations is:
    A. Can it be simplified?
    B. Is it necessary?
    C. Is it performed in proper order or should its position in the procedure be changed?
    D. Is the equipment for doing it satisfactory?

28. You are assigned in charge of a clerical bureau performing a single operation. All five of your subordinates do exactly the same work. A fine spirit of cooperation has developed and the employees help each other and pool their completed work so that the work of any one employee is indistinguishable. Your office is very busy and all five clerks are doing a full day's work. However, reports come back to you from other offices that they are finding as much as 1% error in the work of your bureau. This is too high a percentage of error. 28.____
    Of the following, the BEST procedure for you to follow is to
    A. check all the work yourself
    B. have a sample of the work of each clerk checked by another clerk
    C. have all work done in your office checked by one of your clerks
    D. identify the work of each clerk in some way

29. You are put in charge of a small office. In order to cover the office during the lunch hour, you assign Employee A to remain in the office between the hours of 12 and 1 P.M. On your return to the office at 12:25 P.M., you note that no one is in the office and that the phone is ringing. You are forced to postpone your 12:30 P.M. luncheon appointment, and to remain in the office until 12:50 P.M. when Employee A returns to the office. 29.____
    The BEST of the following actions is:
    A. Ask Employee why he left the office
    B. Bring charges against Employee A for insubordination and neglect of duty
    C. Ignore the matter in your conversation with Employee A so as not to embarrass him
    D. Make a note to rate Employee A low on his service rating

30. You are assigned in charge of a large division. It had been the practice in that division for the employees to slip out for breakfast about 10:00 A.M. You had been successful in stopping this practice and for one week no one had gone out for breakfast. One day a stenographer comes over to you at 10:30 A.M. appearing to be ill. She states that she doesn't feel well and that she would like to go out for a cup of tea. She asks your permission to leave the office for a few minutes. 30.____
You should
   A. telephone and have a cup of tea delivered to her
   B. permit her to go out
   C. refuse her permission to go out inasmuch as this would be setting a bad example
   D. tell her she can leave for an early lunch hour

31. The following four remarks from a supervisor to a subordinate deal with different situations. One remark, however, implies a basically POOR supervisory practice. 31.____
Select this remark as your answer.
   A. "I've called the staff together primarily because I am displeased with the work which one of you is doing. John, don't you think you should be ashamed that you are spoiling the good work of the office?"
   B. "James, you have been with us for six months now. In general, I'm satisfied with your work. However, don't you think you could be more neat in your appearance? I also want you to try to be more accurate in your work."
   C. "Joe, when I assigned this job to you, I did it because it requires special care and I think you're one of our best men in this type of work, but here is a slip-up you've made that we should be especially careful to watch out for in the future."
   D. "Tim, first I'd like to tell you that, effective tomorrow, you are to be my assistant and will receive an increase in salary. Although I recommended you for this position because I felt that you are the best man for the job, there are some things about your work which could stand a bit of improvement. For instance, your manner with regard to visitors is not so polite as it could be."

32. Of the following, the BEST type of floor surface for an office is 32.____
   A. concrete B. hardwood C. linoleum D. parquet

33. The GENERALLY accepted unit for the measurement of illumination at a desk or work bench is the 33.____
   A. ampere B. foot-candle C. volt D. watt

34. The one of the following who is MOST closely allied with "scientific management" is 34.____
   A. Mosher B. Probst C. Taylor D. White

35. Eliminating slack in work assignments is 35.____
A. speed-up
B. time study
C. motion study
D. efficient management

36. "Time studies" examine and measure 36.____
A. past performance
B. present performance
C. long-run effect
D. influence of change

37. The maximum number of subordinates who can be effectively supervised by one supervisor is BEST considered as 37.____
A. determined by the law of "span of control"
B. determined by the law of "span of attention"
C. determined by the type of work supervised
D. fixed at not more than six

38. In the theory and practice of public administration, the one of the following which is LEAST generally regarded as a staff function is 38.____
A. budgeting
B. firefighting
C. purchasing
D. research and information

39. Suppose you are part of an administrative structure in which the executive head has regularly reporting directly to him seventeen subordinates. To some of the subordinates there regularly report directly three employees, to others four employees, and to the remaining subordinates five employees. 39.____
Called upon to make a suggestion concerning this organization, you would question FIRST the desirability of
A. so large a variation among the number of employees regularly reporting directly to subordinates
B. having so large a number of subordinates regularly reporting directly to the administrative head
C. so small a variation among the number of employees regularly reporting directly to subordinates
D. the hierarchical arrangement

40. Administration is the center but not necessarily the source of all ideas for procedural improvement. 40.____
The MOST significant implication that this principle bears for the administrative officer is that
A. before procedural improvements are introduced, they should be approved by a majority of the staff
B. it is the unique function of the administrative officer to derive and introduce procedural improvements
C. the administrative office should derive ideas and suggestions for procedural improvement from all possible sources, introducing any that promise to be effective
D. the administrative officer should view employee grievances as the chief source of procedural improvements

41. The merit system should not end with the appointment of a candidate. In any worthy public service system there should be no dead-end jobs. If the best citizen is to be attracted to public service, there must be provided encouragement and incentive to enable such a career employee to progress in the service. 41.____
The one of the following which is the MOST accurate statement on the basis of the above statement is that
   A. merit system selection has replaced political appointment in many governmental units
   B. lack of opportunities for advancement in government employment will discourage the better qualified from applying
   C. employees who want to progress in the public service should avoid simple assignments
   D. most dead-end jobs have been eliminated from the public service

42. Frequently the importance of keeping office records is not appreciated until information which is badly needed cannot be found. Office records must be kept in convenient and legible form, and must be filed where they may be found quickly. Many clerks are required for this work in large offices and fixed standards of accomplishment often can and must be utilized to get the desired results without loss of time. 42.____
The one of the following which is the MOST accurate statement on the basis of the above statement is:
   A. In setting up a filing system, the system to be used is secondary to the purpose it is to serve.
   B. Office records to be valuable must be kept in duplicate.
   C. The application of work standards to certain clerical functions frequently leads to greater efficiency.
   D. The keeping of office records becomes increasingly important as the business transacted by an office grows.

43. The difference between the average worker and the expert in any occupation is to a large degree a matter of training, yet the difference in their output is enormous. Despite this fact, there are many offices which do not have any organized system of training. 43.____
The MOST accurate of the following statements on the basis of the above statement is that
   A. job training, to be valuable, should be a continuous process
   B. most clerks have the same general intelligence but differ only in the amount of training they have received
   C. skill in an occupation can be acquired as a result of instruction by others
   D. employees with similar training will produce similar quality and quantity of work

44. Sometimes the term "clerical work" is used synonymously with the term "office work" to indicate that the work is clerical work, whether done by a clerk in a place called "the office," by the foreman in the shop, or by an investigator in the field. The essential feature is the work itself, not who does it or where it is done. If it is clerical work in one place, it is clerical work everywhere. 44.____

Of the following, the LEAST DIRECT implication of the above statement is that
A. many jobs have clerical aspects
B. some clerical work is done in offices
C. the term "clerical work" is used in place of the term "office work" to emphasize the nature of the work done rather than by whom it is done
D. clerks are not called upon to perform other than clerical work

45. Scheduling work within a unit involves the knowledge of how long the component parts of the routine take, and the precedence which certain routines should take over others. Usually, the important functions should be attended to on a schedule, and less important work can be handled as fill-in. 45.____
The one of the following which is the VALID statement on the basis of the above statement is that
A. only employees engaged in routine assignments should have their work scheduled
B. the work of an employee should be so scheduled that occasional absences will not upset his routine
C. a proper scheduling of work takes the importance of the various functions of a unit into consideration
D. if office work is not properly scheduled, important functions will be neglected

46. A filing system is unquestionably an effective tool for the systematic executive, and it use in office practice is indispensable, but a casual examination of almost any filing drawer in any office will show that hundreds of letters and papers which have no value whatever are being preserved. 46.____
The LEAST accurate of the following statements on the basis of the above statement is that
A. it is generally considered to be good office practice to destroy letters or papers which are of no value
B. many files are cluttered with useless paper
C. a filing system is a valuable aid in effective office management
D. every office executive should personally make a thorough examination of the files at regular intervals

47. As a supervisor, you may receive requests for information which you know should not be divulged. 47.____
Of the following replies you may give to such a request received over the telephone, the BEST one is:
A. "I regret to advise you that it is the policy of the department not to give out this information over the telephone."
B. "If you hold on a moment, I'll have you connected with the chief of the division."
C. "I am sorry that I cannot help you, but we are not permitted to give out any information regarding such matters."
D. "I am sorry but I know nothing regarding this matter."

48. Training promotes cooperation and teamwork, and results in lowered unit costs of operation. 48.____
The one of the following which is the MOST valid implication of the above statement is that
   A. training is of most value to new employees
   B. training is a factor in increasing efficiency and morale
   C. the actual cost of training employees may be small
   D. training is unnecessary in offices where personnel costs cannot be reduced

49. A government employee should understand how his particular duties contribute to the achievement of the objectives of his department. 49.____
This statement means MOST NEARLY that
   A. an employee who understands the functions of his department will perform his work efficiently
   B. all employees contribute equally in carrying out the objectives of their department
   C. an employee should realize the significance of his work in relation to the aims of his department
   D. all employees should be able to assist in setting up the objectives of a department

50. Many office managers have a tendency to overuse form letters and are prone to print form letters for every occasion, regardless of the number of copies of these letters which is needed. 50.____
On the basis of this statement, it is MOST logical to state that the determination of the need for a form letter should depend upon the
   A. length of the period during which the form letter may be used
   B. number of form letters presently being used in the office
   C. frequency with which the form letter may be used
   D. number of typists who may use the form letter

KEY (CORRECT ANSWERS)

1.	A	11.	B	21.	B	31.	A	41.	B
2.	C	12.	A	22.	B	32.	C	42.	C
3.	C	13.	D	23.	A	33.	B	43.	C
4.	B	14.	A	24.	A	34.	C	44.	D
5.	A	15.	D	25.	D	35.	D	45.	C
6.	A	16.	B	26.	D	36.	B	46.	D
7.	B	17.	B	27.	B	37.	C	47.	C
8.	D	18.	C	28.	D	38.	B	48.	B
9.	B	19.	C	29.	A	39.	B	49.	C
10.	D	20.	D	30.	B	40.	C	50.	C

TEST 2

DIRECTIONS: Each question or incomplete statement is followed by several suggested answers or completions. Select the one that BEST answers the question or completes the statement. *PRINT THE LETTER OF THE CORRECT ANSWER IN THE SPACE AT THE RIGHT.*

1. Your bureau is assigned an important task. 1.____
Of the following, the function that you, as an administrative officer, can LEAST reasonably be expected to perform under these circumstances is the
   A. division of the large job into individual tasks
   B. establishment of "production lines" within the bureau
   C. performance personally of a substantial share of all the work
   D. checkup to see that the work has been well done

2. Suppose that you have broken a complex job into its smaller components before making assignments to the employees under your jurisdiction. 2.____
Of the following, the LEAST advisable procedure to follow from that point is to
   A. give each employee a picture of the importance of his work for the success of the total job
   B. establish a definite line of work flow and responsibility
   C. post a written memorandum of the best method for performing each job
   D. teach a number of alternative methods for doing each job

3. As an administrative officer, you are requested to draw up an organization chart of the whole department. 3.____
Of the following, the MOST important characteristic of such a chart is that it will
   A. include all details of the organization which distinguish it from any other
   B. be a schematic representation of purely administrative functions within the department
   C. present a modification of the actual departmental organization in light of principles of scientific management
   D. present an accurate picture of the lines of authority and responsibility

4. Of the following, the MOST important principle in respect to delegation of authority that should guide you in your work as supervisor in charge of a bureau is that you should 4.____
   A. delegate as much authority as you effectively can
   B. make certain that all administrative details clear through your desk
   C. have all decisions confirmed by you
   D. discourage the practice of consulting you on matters of basic policy

5. Of the following, the LEAST valid criterion to be applied in evaluating the organization of the department in which you are employed as a supervisor is: 5.____
   A. Is authority for making decisions centralized?
   B. Is authority for formulating policy centralized?
   C. Is authority granted commensurate with the responsibility involved?
   D. Is each position and its relation to other positions from the standpoint of responsibility clearly defined?

6. Functional centralization is the bringing together of employees doing the same kind of work and performing similar tasks. 6.____
Of the following, the one which is NOT an important advantage flowing from the introduction of functional centralization in a large city department is that
   A. inter-bureau communication and traffic are reduced
   B. standardized work procedures are introduced more easily
   C. evaluation of employee performances is facilitated
   D. inequalities in working conditions are reduced

7. As a supervisor, you find that a probationary employee under your supervision is consistently below a reasonable standard of performance for the job he is assigned to do. 7.____
Of the following, the MOST appropriate action for you to take FIRST is to
   A. give him an easier job to do
   B. advise him to transfer to another department
   C. recommend to your superior that he be discouraged at the end of his probationary period
   D. determine whether the cause for his below-standard performance can be readily remedied

8. Certain administrative functions, such as those concerned with budgetary and personnel selection activities, have been delegated to central agencies separated from the operating departments. 8.____
Of the following, the PRINCIPAL reason for such separation is that
   A. a central agency is generally better able to secure funds for performing these functions
   B. decentralization increases executive control
   C. greater economy, efficiency, and uniformity can be obtained by establishing central staff of experts to perform these functions
   D. the problems involved in performing these functions vary significantly from one operating department to another

9. The one of the following which is LEAST valid as a guiding principle for you, in your work as supervisor, in building team spirit and teamwork in your bureau is that you should attempt to 9.____
   A. convince the personnel of the bureau that public administration is a worthwhile endeavor
   B. lead every employee to visualize the integration of his own individual function with the program of the whole bureau
   C. develop a favorable public attitude toward the work of the bureau
   D. maintain impartiality by convenient delegation of authority in controversial matters

10. Of the following, the LEAST desirable procedure for the competent supervisor to follow is to 10.____
   A. organize his work before taking responsibility for helping others with theirs
   B. avoid schedules and routines when he is busy
   C. be flexible in planning and carrying out his responsibilities
   D. secure the support of his staff in organizing the total job of the unit

11. The responsibility for making judgment about staff members which is inherent in the supervisor's position may arouse hostilities toward the supervisor. Of the following, the BEST suggestion to the supervisor for handling this responsibility is for the supervisor to avoid 11.____
    A. individual criticism by taking up problems directly through group meetings
    B. any personal feeling or action that would imply that the supervisor has any power over the staff
    C. making critical judgments without accompanying them with reassurance to the staff member concerned

12. To carry out MOST effectively his responsibility for holding to a standard of quantity and quality, the supervisor should 12.____
    A. demand much more from himself than he does from his staff
    B. provide a clearly defined statement of what is expected of the staff
    C. teach the staff to assume responsible attitudes
    D. help the staff out when they get into unavoidable difficulties

13. The supervisor should inspire confidence and respect. This objective is MOST likely to be attained by the supervisor if he endeavors always to 13.____
    A. know the answers to the workers' questions
    B. be fair and just
    C. know what is going on in the office
    D. behave like a supervisor

14. Two chief reasons for the centralization of office functions are to eliminate costly duplication and to bring about greater coordination. The MOST direct implication of this statement is that 14.____
    A. greater coordination of office work will result in centralization of office functions
    B. where there is no centralization of office functions, there can be no coordination of work
    C. centralization of office functions may reduce duplication of work
    D. decentralization of office functions may be a result of costly duplication

15. The efficient administrative assistant arranges a definite schedule of the regular work of his division, but assigns the occasional and emergency tasks when they arise to the employees available at the time to handle these tasks. The management procedure described in this statement is desirable MAINLY because it 15.____
    A. relieves the administrative assistant of the responsibility of supervising the work of his staff
    B. enables more of the staff to become experienced in handling different types of problems
    C. enables the administrative assistant to anticipate problems which may arise
    D. provides for consideration of current work load when making special assignments

16. Well-organized training courses for office employees are regarded by most administrators as a fundamental and essential part of a well-balanced personnel program. 16.____
Such training of clerical employees results LEAST directly in
   A. providing a reservoir of trained employees who can carry on the duties of other clerks during the absence of these clerks
   B. reducing the individual differences in the innate ability of clerical employees to perform complex duties
   C. bringing about a standardization throughout the department of operational methods found to be highly effective in one of its units
   D. preparing clerical employees for promotion to more responsible positions

17. The average typing speed of a typist is not necessarily a true indication of her efficiency. 17.____
Of the following, the BEST justification for this statement is that
   A. the typist may not maintain her maximum typing speed at all times
   B. a rapid typist will ordinarily type more letters than a slow one
   C. a typist's assignments usually include other operations in addition to actual typing
   D. typing speed has no significant relationship to the difficulty of material being typed

18. Although the use of labor-saving machinery and the simplification of procedures tend to decrease unit clerical labor costs, there is, nevertheless, a contrary tendency in the overall cost of office work. This contrary tendency, evidenced by the increase in size of the office staffs, has developed from the increasingly extensive use of systems of analysis and methods of research. 18.____
Of the following, the MOST accurate statement on the basis of the above statement is that
   A. the tendency for the overall costs of office work to increase is bringing about a counter-tendency to decrease unit costs of office work
   B. office machines are of little value in reducing the unit costs of the work of offices in which the overall costs are increasing
   C. The increasing use of systems of analysis and methods of research is bringing about a condition which will necessitate a curtailment of the use of these techniques in the office
   D. expanded office functions tend to offset savings resulting from increased efficiency in office management

19. The most successful supervisor wins his victories through preventive rather than through curative action. 19.____
The one of the following which is the MOST accurate statement on the basis of this statement is that
   A. success in supervision may be measured more accurately in terms of errors corrected than in terms of errors prevented
   B. anticipating problems makes for better supervision than waiting until these problems arise

C. difficulties that cannot be prevented by the supervisor cannot be overcome
D. the solution of problems in supervision is best achieved by scientific methods

20. Assume that you have been requested to design an office form which is to be duplicated by the mimeograph process. 20.____
In planning the layout of the various items appearing on the form, it is LEAST important for you to know the
A. amount of information which the form is to contain
B. purpose for which the form will be used
C. size of the form
D. number of copies of the form which are required

21. The supervisor is responsible for the accuracy of the work performed by her subordinates. 21.____
Of the following procedures which she might adopt to insure the accurate copying of long reports from rough draft originals, the MOST effective one is to
A. examine the rough draft for errors in grammar, punctuation, and spelling before assigning it to a typist to copy
B. glance through each typed report before it leaves her bureau to detect any obvious errors made by the typist
C. have another employee read the rough draft original to the typist who typed the report, and have the typist make whatever corrections are necessary
D. rotate assignments involving the typing of long reports equally among all the typists in the unit

22. The total number of errors made during the month, or other period studied, indicates, in a general way, whether the work has been performed with reasonable accuracy. However, this is not in itself a true measure, but must be considered in relation to the total volume of work produced. 22.____
On the basis of this statement, the accuracy of work performed is MOST truly measured by the
A. total number of errors made during a specified period
B. comparison of the number of errors made and the quantity of work produced during a specified period
C. average amount of work produced by the unit during each month or other designated period of time
D. none of the above answers

23. In the course of your duties, you receive a letter which, you believe, should be called to the attention of your supervisor. 23.____
Of the following, the BEST reason for attaching previous correspondence to this letter before giving it to your supervisor is that
A. there is less danger, if such a procedure is followed, of misplacing important letters
B. this letter can probably be better understood in the light of previous correspondence

C. your supervisor is probably in a better position to understand the letter than you
D. this letter will have to be filed eventually so there is no additional work involved

24. Suppose that you are requested to transmit to the stenographers in your bureau an order curtailing certain privileges that they have been enjoying. You anticipate that your staff may resent curtailment of such privileges. 24.____
Of the following, the BEST action for you to take is to
A. impress upon your staff that an order is an order and must be obeyed
B. attempt to explain to your staff the probable reasons for curtailing their privileges
C. excuse the curtailment of privileges by saying that the welfare of the staff was evidently not considered
D. warn your staff that violation of an order may be considered sufficient cause for immediate dismissal

25. Suppose that a stenographer recently appointed to your bureau submits a memorandum suggesting a change in office procedure that has been tried before and has been found unsuccessful. 25.____
Of the following, the BEST action for you to take is to
A. send the stenographer a note acknowledging receipt of the suggestion, but do not attempt to carry out the suggestion
B. point out that suggestions should come from her supervisor, who has a better knowledge of the problems of the office
C. try out the suggested change a second time, lest the stenographer lose interest in her work
D. call the stenographer in, explain that the change if not practicable, and compliment her for her interest and alertness

26. Suppose that you are assistant to one of the important administrators in your department. You receive a note from the head of department asking your supervisor to assist with a pressing problem that has arisen by making an immediate recommendation. Your supervisor is out of town on official business for a few days and cannot be reached. The head of department, evidently, is not aware of his absence. 26.____
Of the following, the BEST action for you to take is to
A. send the note back to the head of department without comment so as not to incriminate your supervisor
B. forward the note to one of the administrators in another division of the department
C. wait until your supervisor returns and bring the note to his attention immediately
D. get in touch with the head of department immediately and inform him that your supervisor is out of town

27. One of your duties may be to estimate the budget of your unit for the next fiscal year. Suppose that you expect no important changes in the work of your unit during the next year. 27.____

Of the following, the MOST appropriate basis for estimating next year's budget is the
  A. average budget of your unit for the last five years
  B. budget of your unit for the current year plus fifty percent to allow for possible expansion
  C. average current budget of units in your department
  D. budget of your unit for the current fiscal year

28. As a supervisor, you should realize that the work of a stenographer ordinarily requires a higher level of intelligence than the work of a typist CHIEFLY because 28.____
  A. the salary range of stenographers is, in most government and business offices, lower than the salary range of typists
  B. greater accuracy and skill is ordinarily required of a typist
  C. the stenographer must understand what is being dictated to enable her to write it out in shorthand
  D. typists are required to do more technical and specialized work

29. Suppose that you are acting as assistant to an important administrator in your department. 29.____
Of the following, the BEST reason for keeping a separate "pending" file of letters to which answers are expected very soon is that
  A. important correspondence should be placed in a separate, readily accessible file
  B. a periodic check of the "pending" file will indicate the possible need for follow-up letters
  C. correspondence is never final, so provision should be made for keeping files open
  D. there is seldom sufficient room in the permanent files to permit filing all letters

30. For a busy executive in a government department, the services of an assistant are valuable and almost indispensable. 30.____
Of the following, the CHIEF value of an assistant PROBABLY lies in her
  A. ability to assume responsibility for making major decisions
  B. familiarity with the general purpose and functions of civil service
  C. special education
  D. familiarity with the work and detail involved in the duties of the executive whom she assists

31. The supervisor should set a good example. 31.____
Of the following, the CHIEF implication of the above statement is that the supervisor should
  A. behave as he expects his workers to behave
  B. know as much about the worker as his workers do
  C. keep his workers informed of what he is doing
  D. keep ahead of his workers

32. Of the following, the LEAST desirable procedure for the competent supervisor to follow is to 32.____
    A. organize his work before taking responsibility for helping others with theirs
    B. avoid schedules and routines when he is busy
    C. be flexible in planning and carrying out his responsibilities
    D. secure the support of his staff in organizing the total job of the unit

33. Evaluation helps the worker by increasing his security. 33.____
    Of the following, the BEST justification for this statement is that
    A. security and growth depend upon knowledge by the worker of the agency's evaluation
    B. knowledge of his evaluation by agency and supervisor will stimulate the worker to better performance
    C. evaluation enables the supervisor and worker to determine the reasons for the worker's strengths and weaknesses
    D. the supervisor and worker together can usually recognize and deal with any worker's insecurity

34. Systematizing for efficiency means MOST NEARLY 34.____
    A. performing an assignment despite all interruptions
    B. leaving difficult assignments until the next day
    C. having a definite time schedule for certain daily duties
    D. trying to do as little work as possible

35. The CHIEF reason for an employee training program is to 35.____
    A. increase the efficiency of the employee's work
    B. train the employee for promotion examinations
    C. to meet and talk with each new employee
    D. to give the supervisor an opportunity to reprimand the employee for his lack of knowledge

36. A supervisor may encourage his subordinates to make suggestions by 36.____
    A. keeping a record of the number of suggestions an employee makes
    B. providing a suggestion box
    C. outlining a list of possible suggestions
    D. giving credit to a subordinate whose suggestion has been accepted and used

37. The statement that accuracy is of greater importation than speed means MOST NEARLY that 37.____
    A. slower work increases employment
    B. fast workers may be inferior workers
    C. there are many varieties of work to do in an office
    D. the slow worker is the most efficient person

38. To print tabular material is always much more expensive than to print straight text. 38.____
It follows MOST NEARLY that
A. the more columns and subdivisions there are in a table, the more expensive is the printing
B. the omission of the number and title from a table reduces printing costs
C. it is always desirable to only print straight text
D. do not print tabular material as it is too expensive

39. If you were required to give service ratings to employees under your supervision, you should consider as MOST important, during the current period, the 39.____
A. personal characteristics and salary and grade of an employee
B. length of service and the volume of work performed
C. previous service rating given him
D. personal characteristics and the quality of work of an employee

40. If a representative committee of employees in a large department is to meet with an administrative officer for the purpose of improving staff relations and of handling grievances, it is BEST that these meetings be held 40.____
A. at regular intervals
B. whenever requested b an aggrieved employee
C. whenever the need arises
D. at the discretion of the administrative officer

41. In order to be best able to teach a newly appointed employee who must learn to do a type of work which is unfamiliar to him, his supervisor should realize that during this first stage in the learning process the subordinate is GENERALLY characterized by 41.____
A. acute consciousness of self
B. acute consciousness of subject matter, with little interest in persons or personalities
C. inertness or passive acceptance of assigned role
D. understanding of problems without understanding of the means of solving them

42. The MOST accurate of the following principles of education and learning for a supervisor to keep in mind when planning a training program for the assistant supervisors under her supervision is that 42.____
A. assistant supervisors, like all other individuals, vary in the rate at which they learn new material and in the degree to which they can retain what they do learn
B. experienced assistant supervisors who have the same basic college education and agency experience will be able to learn new material at approximately the same rate of speed
C. the speed with which assistant supervisors can learn new material after the age of forty is half as rapid as at ages twenty to thirty
D. with regard to any specific task, it is easier and takes less time to break an experienced assistant supervisor of old, unsatisfactory work habits than it is to teach him new, acceptable ones

43. A supervisor has been transferred from supervision of one group of units to another group of units in the same center. She spends the first three weeks in her new assignment in getting acquainted with her new subordinates, their caseload problems and their work. In this process, she notices that some of the cash records and forms which are submitted to her by two of the assistant supervisors are carelessly or improperly prepared. 43.____
The BEST of the following actions for the supervisor to take in this situation is to
A. carefully check the work submitted by these assistant supervisors during an additional three weeks before taking any more positive action
B. confer with these offending workers and show each one where her work needs improvement and how to go about achieving it
C. institute an in-service training program specifically designed to solve such a problem and instruct the entire subordinate staff in proper work methods
D. make a note of these errors for documentary use in preparing the annual service rating reports and advise the workers involved to prepare their work more carefully

44. A supervisor, who was promoted to this position a year ago, has supervised a certain assistant supervisor for this one year. The work of the assistant supervisor has been very poor because he has done a minimum of work, refused to take sufficient responsibility, been difficult to handle, and required very close supervision. Apparently due to the increasing insistence by his supervisor that he improve the caliber of his work, the assistant supervisor tenders his resignation, stating that the demands of the job are too much for him. The opinion of the previous supervisor, who had supervised this assistant supervisor for two years, agrees substantially with that of the new supervisor. 44.____
Under such circumstances, the BEST of the following actions the supervisor can take, in general, is to
A. recommend that the resignation be accepted and that he be rehired should he later apply when he feels able to do the job
B. recommend that the resignation be accepted and that he not be rehired should he later so apply
C. refuse to accept the resignation but try to persuade the assistant supervisor to accept psychiatric help
D. refuse to accept the resignation, promising the assistant supervisor that he will be less closely supervised in the future since he is now so experienced

45. Rumors have arisen to the effect that one of the staff investigators under your supervision has been attending classes at a local university during afternoon hours when he is supposed to be making field visits. 45.____
The BEST of the following ways for you to approach this problem is to
A. disregard the rumors since, like most rumors, they probably have no actual foundation in fact
B. have a discreet investigation made in order to determine the actual facts prior to taking any other action

C. inform the investigator that you know what he has been doing and that such behavior is overt dereliction of duty and is punishable by dismissal
D. review the investigator's work record, spot check his cases, and take no further action unless the quality of his work is below average for the unit

46. A supervisor must consider many factors in evaluating a worker whom he has supervised for a considerable time. 46.____
In evaluating the capacity of such a worker to use independent judgment, the one of the following to which the supervisor should generally give MOST consideration is the worker's
A. capacity to establish good relationships with people (clients, colleagues)
B. educational background
C. emotional stability
D. the quality and judgment shown by the worker in previous work situations known to the supervisor

47. A supervisor is conducting a special meeting with the assistant supervisors under her supervision to read and discuss some major complex changes in the rules and procedures. She notices that one of the assistant supervisors who is normally attentive at meetings seems to be paying no attention to what is being said. The supervisor stops reading the rules and asks the assistant supervisor a couple of questions about the changed procedure, to which she gets satisfactory answers. 47.____
The BEST action of the following for the supervisor to take at the meeting is to
A. advise the assistant supervisor gently but firmly that these changes are complex and that her undivided attention is required in order to fully comprehend them
B. avoid further embarrassment to the assistant supervisor by asking the group as a whole to pay more attention to what is being read
C. discontinue the questioning and resume reading the procedure
D. politely request the assistant supervisor to stop giving those present the impression that she is uninterested in what goes on about her

48. A supervisor becomes aware that one of her very competent experienced workers never takes notes during an interview with a client except to note an occasional name, address, or date. When asked about this practice by the supervisor, the worker states that she has a good memory for important details and has always been able to satisfactorily record an interview after the client has left. 48.____
It would generally be BEST for the supervisor to handle this situation by
A. discussing with her that more extensive note-taking may sometimes be desirable with a client who believes note-taking to be evidence that his problem will receive serious consideration
B. agreeing with this practice since note-taking interferes with the establishment of a proper worker-client relationship
C. explaining that, since interviewing is an art form rather than an exact science, a good worker must devise her own personal rules for interviewing and not be bound by general principles

D. warning the worker that memory is too uncertain a thing to be relied upon and, therefore, notes should be taken during an interview of all matters

49. When an experienced subordinate who has the authority and information necessary to make a decision on a certain difficult matter brings the matter to his supervisor without having made the decision, it would generally be BEST for the supervisor to 49.____
   A. agree to make the decision for the subordinate after the subordinate has explained why he finds it difficult to make the decision and after he has made a recommendation
   B. make the decision for the subordinate, explaining to him the reasons for arriving at the decision
   C. refuse to make the decision, but discuss the various alternatives with the subordinate in order to clarify the issues involved
   D. refuse to make the decision, explaining to the subordinate that he is deemed to be fully qualified and competent to make the decision

50. The one of the following instances when it is MOST important for an upper level supervisor to follow the chain of command is when he is 50.____
   A. communicating decisions
   B. communicating information
   C. receiving suggestions
   D. seeking information

KEY (CORRECT ANSWERS)

1.	C	11.	D	21.	C	31.	A	41.	A
2.	D	12.	B	22.	B	32.	B	42.	A
3.	D	13.	B	23.	B	33.	C	43.	B
4.	A	14.	C	24.	B	34.	C	44.	B
5.	D	15.	D	25.	D	35.	A	45.	B
6.	A	16.	B	26.	D	36.	D	46.	D
7.	D	17.	C	27.	D	37.	B	47.	C
8.	C	18.	D	28.	C	38.	A	48.	A
9.	D	19.	B	29.	B	39.	D	49.	C
10.	B	20.	D	30.	D	40.	A	50.	A

TEST 3

DIRECTIONS: Each question or incomplete statement is followed by several suggested answers or completions. Select the one that BEST answers the question or completes the statement. *PRINT THE LETTER OF THE CORRECT ANSWER IN THE SPACE AT THE RIGHT.*

1. Experts in the field of personnel relations feel that it is generally bad practice for subordinate employees to become aware of pending or contemplated changes in policy or organizational set-up via the "grapevine" CHIEFLY because 1.____
   A. evidence that one or more responsible officials have proved untrustworthy will undermine confidence in the agency
   B. the information disseminated by this method is seldom entirely accurate and generally spreads needless unrest among the subordinate staff
   C. the subordinate staff may conclude that the administration feels the staff cannot be trusted with the true information
   D. the subordinate staff may conclude that the administration lacks the courage to make an unpopular announcement through officials channels

2. In order to maintain a proper relationship with a worker who is assigned to staff rather than line functions, a line supervisor should 2.____
   A. accept all recommendations of the staff worker
   B. include the staff worker in the conferences called by the supervisor for his subordinates
   C. keep the staff worker informed of developments in the area of his staff assignment
   D. require that the staff worker's recommendations be communicated to the supervisor through the supervisor's own superior

3. Of the following, the GREATEST disadvantage of placing a worker in a staff position under the direct supervision of the supervisor whom he advises is the possibility that the 3.____
   A. staff worker will tend to be insubordinate because of a feeling of superiority over the supervisor
   B. staff worker will tend to give advice of the type which the supervisor wants to hear or finds acceptable
   C. supervisor will tend to be mistrustful of the advice of a worker of subordinate rank
   D. supervisor will tend to derive little benefit from the advice because to supervise properly he should know at least as much as his subordinate

4. One factor which might be given consideration in deciding upon the optimum span of control of a supervisor over his immediate subordinates is the position of the supervisor in the hierarchy of the organization. It is generally considered proper that the number of subordinates immediately supervised by a higher, upper echelon, supervisor 4.____
   A. is unrelated to and tends to form no pattern with the number supervised by lower level supervisors
   B. should be about the same as the number supervised by a lower level supervisor

C. should be larger than the number supervised by a lower level supervisor
D. should be smaller than the number supervised by a lower level supervisor

5. An important administrative problem is how precisely to define the limits on authority that is delegated to subordinate supervisors. 5.____
Such definition of limits of authority should be
A. as precise as possible and practicable in all areas
B. as precise as possible and practicable in areas of function, but should allow considerable flexibility in the area of personnel management
C. as precise as possible and practicable in the area of personnel management, but should allow considerable flexibility in the areas of function
D. in general terms so as to allow considerable flexibility both in the areas of function and in the areas of personnel management

6. The LEAST important of the following reasons why a particular activity should be assigned to a unit which performs activities dissimilar to it is that 6.____
A. close coordination is needed between the particular activity and other activities performed by the unit
B. it will enhance the reputation and prestige of the unit supervisor
C. the unit makes frequent use of the results of this particular activity
D. the unit supervisor has a sound knowledge and understanding of the particular activity

7. A supervisor is put in charge of a special unit. She is exceptionally well-qualified for this assignment by her training and experience. One of her very close personal friends has been working for some time as a field investigator in this unit. Both the supervisor and investigator are certain that the rest of the investigators in the unit, many of whom have been in the bureau for a long time, know of this close relationship. 7.____
Under these circumstances, the MOST advisable action for the supervisor to take is to
A. ask that either she be allowed to return to her old assignment, or, if that cannot be arranged, that her friend be transferred to another unit in the center
B. avoid any overt sign of favoritism by acting impartially and with greater reserve when dealing with this investigator than the rest of the staff
C. discontinue any socializing with this investigator either inside or outside the office so as to eliminate any gossip or dissatisfaction
D. talk the situation over with the other investigators and arrive at a mutually acceptable plan of proper office decorum

8. The one of the following causes of clerical error which is usually considered to be LEAST attributable to faulty supervision or inefficient management is 8.____
A. inability to carry out instructions
B. too much work to do
C. an inappropriate record-keeping system
D. continual interruptions

9. Assume that you are the supervisor of a clerical unit in a government agency. One of your subordinates violates a rule of the agency, a violation which requires that the employee be suspended from his work for one day. The violated rule is one that you have found to be unduly strict and you have recommended to the management of the agency that the rule be changed or abolished. The management has been considering your recommendation but has not yet reached a decision on the matter. 9.____
In these circumstances, you should
   A. not initiate disciplinary action, but, instead explain to the employee that the rule may be changed shortly
   B. delay disciplinary action on the violation until the management has reached a decision on changing the rule
   C. modify the disciplinary action by reprimanding the employee and informing him that further action may be taken when the management has reached a decision on changing the rule
   D. initiate the prescribed disciplinary action without commenting on the strictness of the rule or on your recommendation

10. Assume that a supervisor praises his subordinates for satisfactory aspects of their work only when he is about to criticize them for unsatisfactory aspects of their work. 10.____
Such a practice is undesirable PRIMARILY because
   A. his subordinates may expect to be praised for their work even if it is unsatisfactory
   B. praising his subordinates for some aspects of their work while criticizing other aspects will weaken the effects of the criticisms
   C. his subordinates would be more receptive to criticism if it were followed by praise
   D. his subordinates may come to disregard praise and wait for criticism to be given

11. The one of the following which would be the BEST reason for an agency to eliminate a procedure for obtaining and recording certain information is that 11.____
   A. it is no longer legally required to obtain the information
   B. there is an advantage in obtaining the information
   C. the information could be compiled on the basis of other information available
   D. the information obtained is sometimes incorrect

12. In determining the type and number of records to be kept in an agency, it is important to recognize that records are of value PRIMARILY as 12.____
   A. raw material to be used in statistical analysis
   B. sources of information about the agency's activities
   C. by-products of the activities carried on by the agency
   D. data for evaluating the effectiveness of the agency

Questions 13-17.

DIRECTIONS: Each of Questions 13 through 17 consists of a statement which contains one word that is incorrectly used because it is not in keeping with the meaning that the statement is evidently intended to convey. For each of these questions, you are to select the incorrectly used word and substitute for it one of the words lettered A, B, C, or D, which helps BEST to convey the meaning of the statement.

13. There has developed in recent years an increasing awareness of the need to measure the quality of management in all enterprises and to seek the principles that can serve as a basis for this improvement. 13.____
A. growth B. raise C. efficiency D. define

14. It is hardly an exaggeration to deny that the permanence, productivity, and humanity of any industrial system depend upon its ability to utilize the positive and constructive impulses of all who work and upon its ability to arouse and continue interest in the necessary activities. 14.____
A. develop B. efficiency C. state D. inspiration

15. The selection of managers on the basis of technical knowledge alone seems to recognize that the essential characteristic of management is getting things done through others, thereby demanding skills that are essential in coordinating the activities of subordinates. 15.____
A. training
B. fails
C. organization
D. improving

16. Only when it is deliberate and when it is clearly understood what impressions the ease of communication will probably create in the minds of employees and subordinate management, should top management refrain from commenting on a subject that is of general concern. 16.____
A. obvious B. benefit C. doubt D. absence

17. Scientific planning of work requires careful analysis of facts and a precise plan of action for the whims and fancies of executives that often provide only a vague indication of work to be done. 17.____
A. substitutes
B. development
C. preliminary
D. comprehensive

18. Assume that you are a supervisor. One of the workers under your supervision is careless about the routine aspects of his work. 18.____
Of the following, the action MOST likely to develop in this worker a better attitude toward job routines is to demonstrate that
A. it is just as easy to do his job the right way
B. organization of his job will leave more time for field work
C. the routine part of the job is essential to performing a good piece of work
D. job routines are a responsibility of the worker

19. A supervisor can MOST effectively secure necessary improvement in a worker's office work by 19.____
    A. encouraging the worker to keep abreast of his work
    B. relating the routine part of his job to the total job to be done
    C. helping the worker to establish a good system for covering his office work and holding him to it
    D. informing the worker that he will be required to organize his work more efficiently

20. A supervisor should offer criticism in such a manner that the criticisms is helpful and not overwhelming. 20.____
    Of the following, the LEAST valid inference that can be drawn on the basis of the above statement is that a supervisor should
    A. demonstrate that the criticism is partial and not total
    B. give criticism in such a way that it does not undermine the worker's self-confidence
    C. keep his relationships with the worker objective
    D. keep criticism directed towards general work performance

21. The one of the following areas in which a worker may LEAST reasonably expect direct assistance from the supervisor is in 21.____
    A. building up rapport with all clients
    B. gaining insight into the unmet needs of clients
    C. developing an understanding of community resources
    D. interpreting agency policies and procedures

22. You are informed that a worker under your supervision has submitted a letter complaining of unfair service rating. 22.____
    Of the following, the MOST valid assumption for you to make concerning this worker is that he should be
    A. more adequately supervised in the future
    B. called in for a supervisory conference
    C. given a transfer to some other unit where he may be more happy
    D. given no more consideration than any other inefficient worker

23. Assume that you are a supervisor. You find that a somewhat bewildered worker, newly appointed to the department, hesitates to ask questions for fear of showing his ignorance and jeopardizing his position. 23.____
    Of the following, the BEST procedure for you to follow is to
    A. try to discover the reason for his evident fear of authority
    B. tell him that when he is in doubt about a procedure or a policy he should consult his fellow workers
    C. develop with the worker a plan for more frequent supervisory conferences
    D. explain why each staff member is eager to give him available information that will help him do a good job

24. Of the following, the MOST effective method of helping a newly-appointed employee adjust to his new job is to 24.____
    A. assure him that with experience his uncertain attitudes will be replaced by a professional approach
    B. help him, by accepting him as he is, to have confidence in his ability to handle the job
    C. help him to be on guard against the development of punitive attitudes
    D. help him to recognize the mutability of the agency's policies and procedures

25. Suppose that, as a supervisor, you have scheduled an individual conference with an experienced employee under your supervision. 25.____
    Of the following, the BEST plan of action for this conference is to
    A. discuss the work that the employee is most interested in
    B. plan with the employee to cover any problems that are difficult for him
    C. advise the employee that the conference is his to do with as he sees fit
    D. spot check the employee's work in advance and select those areas for discussion in which the employee has done poor work

26. Of the following, the CHIEF function of a supervisor should be to 26.____
    A. assist in the planning of new policies and the evaluation of existing ones
    B. promote congenial relationships among members of the staff
    C. achieve optimum functioning of each unit and each worker
    D. promote the smooth functioning of job routines

27. The competent supervisor must realize the importance of planning. 27.____
    Of the following, the aspect of planning which is LEAST appropriately considered a responsibility of the supervisor is
    A. long-range planning for the proper functioning of his unit
    B. planning to take care of peak and slack periods
    C. planning to cover agency policies in group conferences
    D. long-range planning to develop community resources

28. The one of the following objectives which should be of LEAST concern to the supervisor in the performance of his duties is to 28.____
    A. help the worker to make friends with all of his fellow employees
    B. be impartial and fair to all members of the staff
    C. stimulate the worker's growth on the job
    D. meet the needs of the individual employee

29. The one of the following which is LEAST properly considered a direct responsibility of the supervisor is 29.____
    A. liaison between the staff and the administrator
    B. interpreting administrative orders and procedures to the employees
    C. training new employees
    D. maintaining staff morale at a high level

30. In order to teach the employee to develop an objective approach, the BEST action for the supervisor to take is to help the worker to 30.____
   A. develop a sincere interest in his job
   B. understand the varied responsibilities that are an integral part of his job
   C. differentiate clearly between himself as a friend and as an employee
   D. find satisfaction in his work

31. If the employee shows excessive submission which indicates a need for dependence on the supervisor in handling an assignment, it would be MOST advisable for the supervisor to 31.____
   A. indicate firmly that the employee-supervisor relationship does not call for submission
   B. define areas of responsibility of employee and supervisor
   C. recognize the employee's need and of supervisor
   D. recognize the employee's need to be sustained and supported and help him by making decisions for him

32. Assume that, as a supervisor, you are conducting a group conference. Of the following, the BEST procedure for you to follow in order to stimulate group discussion is to 32.____
   A. permit the active participation of all members
   B. direct the discussion to an acceptable conclusion
   C. resolve conflicts of opinion among members of the group
   D. present a question for discussion on which the group members have some knowledge or experience

33. Suppose that, as a new supervisor, you wish to inform the staff under your supervision of your methods of operation. Of the following, the BEST procedure for you to follow is to 33.____
   A. advise the staff that they will learn gradually from experience
   B. inform each employee in an individual conference
   C. call a group conference for this purpose
   D. distribute a written memorandum among all members of the staff

34. The MOST constructive and effective method of correcting an employee who has made a mistake is, in general, to 34.____
   A. explain that his evaluation is related to his errors
   B. point out immediately where he erred and tell him how it should have been done
   C. show him how to readjust his methods so as to avoid similar errors in the future
   D. try to discover by an indirect method why the error was made

35. The MOST effective method for the supervisor to follow in order to obtain the cooperation of an employee under his supervision is, wherever possible, to 35.____
   A. maintain a careful record of performance in order to keep the employee on his toes
   B. give the employee recognition in order to promote greater effort and give him more satisfaction in his work

C. try to gain the employee's cooperation for the good of the service
D. advise the employee that his advancement on the job depends on his cooperation

36. Of the following, the MOST appropriate initial course for an employee to take when he is unable to clarify a policy with his supervisor is to 36.____
A. bring up the problem at the next group conference
B. discuss the policy immediately with his fellow employees
C. accept the supervisor's interpretation as final
D. determine what responsibility he has for putting the policy into effect

37. Good administration allows for different treatment of different workers. 37.____
Of the following, the CHIEF implication of this statement is that
A. it would be unfair for the supervisor not to treat all staff members alike
B. fear of favoritism tends to undermine staff morale
C. best results are obtained by individualization within the limits of fair treatment
D. difficult problems call for a different kind of approach

38. The MOST effective and appropriate method of building efficiency and morale in a group of employees is, in general, 38.____
A. by stressing the economic motive
B. through use of the authority inherent in the position
C. by a friendly approach to all
D. by a discipline that is fair but strict

39. Of the following, the LEAST valid basis for the assignment of work to an employee is the 39.____
A. kind of service to be rendered
B. experience and training of the employee
C. health and capacity of the employee
D. racial composition of the community where the office is located

40. The CHIEF justification for staff education, consisting of in-service training, lies in its contribution to 40.____
A. improvement in the quality of work performed
B. recruitment of a better type of employee
C. employee morale, accruing from a feeling of growth on the job
D. the satisfaction that the employee gets on his job

41. Suppose that you are a supervisor. An employee no longer with your department requests you, as his former supervisor, to write a letter recommending him for a position with a private organization. 41.____
Of the following the BEST procedure for you to follow is to include in the letter only information that
A. will help the applicant get the job
B. is clear, factual, and substantiated
C. is known to you personally
D. can readily be corroborated by personal interview

42. Of the following, the MOST important item on which to base the efficiency evaluation of an employee under your supervision is 32.____
   A. the nature of the relationship that he has built up with his fellow employees
   B. how he gets along with his supervisors
   C. his personal habits and skills
   D. the effectiveness of his control over his work

43. According to generally accepted personnel practice, the MOST effective method of building morale in a new employee is to 43.____
   A. exercise caution in praising the employee, lest he become overconfident
   B. give sincere and frank recommendation whenever possible in order to stimulate interest and effort
   C. praise the employee highly even for mediocre performance so that he will be stimulated to do better
   D. warn the employee frequently that he cannot hope to succeed unless he puts forth his best efforts

44. Errors made by newly-appointed employees often follow a predictable pattern. The one of the following errors likely to have LEAST serious consequences is the tendency of a new employee to 44.____
   A. discuss problems that are outside his province with the client
   B. persuade the client to accept the worker's solution of a problem
   C. be two strict in carrying out departmental policy and procedure
   D. depend upon the use of authority due to his inexperience and lack of skill in working with people

45. The MOST effective way for a supervisor to break down a worker's defensive stand against supervisory guidance is to 45.____
   A. come to an understanding with him on the mutual responsibilities involved in the job of the employee and that of the supervisor
   B. tell him he must feel free to express his opinions and to discuss basic problems
   C. show him how to develop toward greater objectivity, sensitivity, and understanding
   D. advise him that it is necessary to carry out agency policy and procedures in order to do a good job

46. Of the following, the LEAST essential function of the supervisor who is conducting a group conference should be to 46.____
   A. keep attention focused on the purpose of the conference
   B. encourage discussion of controversial points
   C. make certain that all possible viewpoints are discussed
   D. be thoroughly prepared in advance

47. When conducting a group conference, the supervisor should be LEAST concerned with 47.____
   A. providing an opportunity for the free interchange of ideas
   B. imparting knowledge and understanding of the work

C. leading the discussion toward a planned goal
D. pointing out where individual workers have erred in work practice

48. If the participants in a group conference are unable to agree on the proper application of a concept to the work of a department, the MOST suitable temporary procedure for the supervisor to follow is to 48.____
A. suggest that each member think the subject through before the next meeting
B. tell the group to examine their differences for possible conflicts with present policies
C. suggest that practices can be changed because of new conditions
D. state the acceptable practice in the agency and whether deviations from such practice can be permitted

49. If an employee is to participate constructively in any group discussion, it is MOST important that he have 49.____
A. advance notice of the agenda for the meeting
B. long experience in the department
C. knowledge and experience in the particular work
D. the ability to assume a leadership role

50. Of the following, the MOST important principle for the supervisor to follow when conducting a group discussion is that he should 50.____
A. move the discussion toward acceptance by the group of a particular point of view
B. express his ideas clearly and succinctly
C. lead the group to accept the authority inherent in his position
D. contribute to the discussion from his knowledge and experience

---

KEY (CORRECT ANSWERS)

1.	B	11.	C	21.	A	31.	B	41.	B
2.	C	12.	B	22.	B	32.	D	42.	D
3.	B	13.	B	23.	C	33.	C	43.	B
4.	D	14.	C	24.	B	34.	C	44.	C
5.	A	15.	B	25.	B	35.	B	45.	A
6.	B	16.	D	26.	C	36.	D	46.	B
7.	A	17.	A	27.	D	37.	C	47.	D
8.	A	18.	D	28.	A	38.	D	48.	D
9.	D	19.	B	29.	A	39.	D	49.	A
10.	D	20.	D	30.	C	40.	A	50.	D

RECORD KEEPING

EXAMINATION SECTION

TEST 1

DIRECTIONS: Each question or incomplete statement is followed by several suggested answers or completions. Select the one that BEST answers the question or completes the statement. *PRINT THE LETTER OF THE CORRECT ANSWER IN THE SPACE AT THE RIGHT.*

Questions 1-15.

DIRECTIONS: Questions 1 through 15 are to be answered on the basis of the following list of company names below. Arrange a file alphabetically, word-by-word, disregarding punctuation, conjunctions, and apostrophes. Then answer the questions.

A Bee C Reading Materials
ABCO Parts
A Better Course for Test Preparation
AAA Auto Parts Co.
A-Z Auto Parts, Inc.
Aabar Books
Abbey, Joanne
Boman-Sylvan Law Firm
BMW Autowerks
C Q Service Company
Chappell-Murray, Inc.
E&E Life Insurance
Emcrisco
Gigi Arts
Gordon, Jon & Associates
SOS Plumbing
Schmidt, J.B. Co.

1. Which of these files should appear FIRST? 1.____
   A. ABCO Parts
   B. A Bee C Reading Materials
   C. A Better Course for Test Preparation
   D. AAA Auto Parts Co.

2. Which of these files should appear SECOND? 2.____
   A. A-Z Auto Parts, Inc.
   B. A Bee C Reading Materials
   C. A Better Course for Test Preparation
   D. AAA Auto Parts Co.

3. Which of these files should appear THIRD? 3.____
   A. ABCO Parts
   B. A Bee C Reading Materials
   C. Aabar Books
   D. AAA Auto Parts Co.

4. Which of these files should appear FOURTH? 4.____
   A. Aabar Books
   B. ABCO Parts
   C. Abbey, Joanne
   D. AAA Auto Parts Co.

5. Which of these files should appear LAST? 5.____
   A. Gordon, Jon & Associates
   B. Gigi Arts
   C. Schmidt, J.B. Co.
   D. SOS Plumbing

6. Which of these files should appear between A-Z Auto Parts, Inc. and Abbey, Joanne? 6.____
   A. A Bee C Reading Materials
   B. AAA Auto Parts Co.
   C. ABCO Parts
   D. A Better Course for Test Preparation

7. Which of these files should appear between ABCO Parts and Aabar Books? 7.____
   A. A Bee C Reading Materials
   B. Abbey, Joanne
   C. Aabar Books
   D. A-Z Auto Parts

8. Which of these files should appear between Abbey, Joanne and Boman-Sylvan Law Firm? 8.____
   A. A Better Course for Test Preparation
   B. BMW Autowerks
   C. Chappell-Murray, Inc.
   D. Aabar Books

9. Which of these files should appear between Abbey, Joanne and C Q Service? 9.____
   A. A-Z Auto Parts, Inc.
   B. BMW Autowerks
   C. Choices A and B
   D. Chappell-Murray, Inc.

10. Which of these files should appear between C Q Service Company and Emcrisco? 10.____
    A. Chappell-Murray, Inc.
    B. E&E Life Insurance
    C. Gigi Arts
    D. Choices A and B

11. Which of these files should NOT appear between C Q Service Company and E&E Life Insurance? 11.____
    A. Gordon, Jon & Associates
    B. Emcrisco
    C. Gigi Arts
    D. All of the above

12. Which of these files should appear between Chappell-Murray, Inc. and Gigi Arts? 12.____
   A. C Q Service Inc., E&E Life Insurance, and Emcrisco
   B. Emcrisco, E&E Life Insurance, and Gordon, Jon & Associates
   C. E&E Life Insurance, and Emcrisco
   D. Emcrisco and Gordon, Jon & Associates

13. Which of these files should appear between Gordon, Jon & Associates and SOS Plumbing? 13.____
   A. Gigi Arts
   B. Schmidt,J.B. Co.
   C. Choices A and B
   D. None of the above

14. Each of the choices lists the four files in their proper alphabetical order EXCEPT 14.____
   A. E&E Life Insurance; Gigi Arts; Gordon, Jon & Associates; SOS Plumbing
   B. E&E Life Insurance; Emcrisco; Gigi Arts; SOS Plumbing
   C. Emcrisco; Gordon, Jon & Associates; SOS Plumbing; Schmidt, J.B. Co.
   D. Emcrisco; Gigi Arts; Gordon, Jon & Associates; SOS Plumbing

15. Which of the choices lists the four files in their proper alphabetical order? 15.____
   A. Gigi Arts; Gordon, Jon & Associates; SOS Plumbing; Schmidt, J.B. Co.
   B. Gordon, Jon & Associates; Gigi Arts; Schmidt, J.B. Co.; SOS Plumbing
   C. Gordon, Jon & Associates; Gigi Arts; SOS Plumbing; Schmidt, J.B. Co.
   D. Gigi Arts; Gordon, Jon & Associates; Schmidt, J.B. Co.; SOS Plumbing

16. The alphabetical filing order of two businesses with identical names is determined by the 16.____
   A. length of time each business has been operating
   B. addresses of the businesses
   C. last name of the company president
   D. no one of the above

17. In an alphabetical filing system, if a business name includes a number, it should be 17.____
   A. disregarded
   B. considered a number and placed at the end of an alphabetical section
   C. treated as though it were written in words and alphabetized accordingly
   D. considered a number and placed at the beginning of an alphabetical section

18. If a business name includes a contraction (such as *don't* or *it's*), how should that word be treated in an alphabetical system? 18.____
   A. Divide the word into its separate parts and treat it as two words
   B. Ignore the letters that come after the apostrophe
   C. Ignore the word that contains the contraction
   D. Ignore the apostrophe and consider all letters in the contraction

19. In what order should the parts of an address be considered when using an alphabetical filing system? 19.____
    A. City or town; state; street name; house or building number
    B. State; city or town; street name; house or building number
    C. House or building number; street name; city or town; state
    D. Street name; city or town; state

20. A business record should be cross-referenced when a(n) 20.____
    A. organization is known by an abbreviated name
    B. business has a name change because of a sale, incorporation, or other reason
    C. business is known by a *coined* or common name which differs from a dictionary spelling
    D. all of the above

21. A geographical filing system is MOST effective when 21.____
    A. location is more important than name
    B. many names or titles sound alike
    C. dealing with companies who have offices all over the world
    D. filing personal and business files

Questions 22-25.

DIRECTIONS: Questions 22 through 25 are to be answered on the basis of the list of items below, which are to be filed geographically. Organize the items geographically and then answer the questions.

I. University Press at Berkeley, U.S.
II. Maria Sanchez, Mexico City, Mexico
III. Great Expectations Ltd. in London, England
IV. Justice League, Cape Town, South Africa, Africa
V. Crown Pearls Ltd. in London, England
VI. Joseph Prasad in London, England

22. Which of the following arrangements of the items is composed according to the policy of: *Continent, Country, City, Firm or Individual Name*? 22.____
    A. V, III, IV, VI, II, I
    B. IV, V, III, VI, II, I
    C. I, IV, V, III, VI, II
    D. IV, V, III, VI, I, II

23. Which of the following files is arranged according to the policy of: *Continent, Country, City, Firm or Individual Name*? 23.____
    A. South Africa; Africa; Cape Town; Justice League
    B. Mexico; Mexico City; Maria Sanchez
    C. North America; United States; Berkeley; University Press
    D. England; Europe; London; Prasad, Joseph

24. Which of the following arrangements of the items is composed according to the policy of: *Country, City, Firm or Individual Name*? 24.____
    A. V, VI, III, II, IV, I
    B. I, V, VI, III, II, IV
    C. VI, V, III, II, IV, I
    D. V, III, VI, II, IV, I

25. Which of the following files is arranged according to a policy of: *Country, City, Firm or Individual Name*? 25.____
    A. England; London; Crown Pearls Ltd.
    B. North America; United States; Berkeley; University Press
    C. Africa; Cape Town; Justice League
    D. Mexico City; Mexico; Maria Sanchez

26. Under which of the following circumstances would a phonetic filing system be MOST effective? 26.____
    A. When the person in charge of filing can't spell very well
    B. With large files with names that sound alike
    C. With large files with names that are spelled alike
    D. All of the above

Questions 27-29.

DIRECTIONS: Questions 27 through 29 are to be answered on the basis of the following list of numerical files.

I. 391-023-100
II. 361-132-170
III. 385-732-200
IV. 381-432-150
V. 391-632-387
VI. 361-423-303
VII. 391-123-271

27. Which of the following arrangements of the files follows a consecutive-digit system? 27.____
    A. II, III, IV, I
    B. I, V, VII, III
    C. II, IV, III, I
    D. III, I, V, VII

28. Which of the following arrangements follows a terminal-digit system? 28.____
    A. I, VII, II, IV, III
    B. II, I, IV, V, VII
    C. VII, VI, V, IV, III
    D. I, IV, II, III, VII

29. Which of the following lists follows a middle-digit system? 29.____
    A. I, VII, II, VI, IV, V, III
    B. I, II, VII, IV, VI, V, III
    C. VII, II, I, III, V, VI, IV
    D. VII, I, II, IV, VI, V, III

Questions 30-31.

DIRECTIONS: Questions 30 and 31 are to be answered on the basis of the following information.

I. Reconfirm Laura Bates appointment with James Caldecort on December 12 at 9:30 A.M.
II. Laurence Kinder contact Julia Lucas on August 3 and set up a meeting for week of September 23 at 4 P.M.
III. John Lutz contact Larry Waverly on August 3 and set up appointment for September 23 at 9:30 A.M.
IV. Call for tickets for Gerry Stanton August 21 for New Jersey on September 23, flight 143 at 4:43 P.M.

30. A chronological file for the above information would be 30.____
A. IV, III, II, I B. III, II, IV, I C. IV, II, III, I D. III, I, II, IV

31. Using the above information, a chronological file for the date September 23 would be 31.____
A. II, III, IV B. III, I, IV C. III, II, IV D. IV, III, II

Questions 32-34.

DIRECTIONS: Questions 32 through 34 are to be answered on the basis of the following information.

I. Call Roger Epstein, Ashoke Naipaul, Jon Anderson, and Sara Washingon on April 19 at 1:00 P.M. to set up meeting with Alika D'Ornay for June 6 in New York.
II. Call Martin Ames before noon on April 19 to confirm afternoon meeting with Bob Greenwood on April 20th.
III. Set up meeting room at noon for 2:30 P.M. meeting on April 19th.
IV. Ashley Stanton contact Bob Greenwood at 9:00 A.M. on April 20 and set up meeting for June 6 at 8:30 A.M.
V. Carol Guiland contact Shelby Van Ness during afternoon of April 20 and set up meeting for June 6 at 10:00 A.M.
VI. Call airline and reserve tickets on June 6 for Roger Epstein trip to Denver on July 8.
VII. Meeting at 2:30 P.M. on April 19th.

32. A chronological file for all of the above information would be 32.____
A. II, I, III, VII, V, IV, VI
B. III, VII, II, I, IV, V, VI
C. III, VII, I, II, V, IV, VI
D. II, III, I, VII, IV, V, VI

33. A chronological file for the date of April 19th would be 33.____
A. II, III, VII, I B. II, III, I, VII C. VII, I, III, II D. III, VII, I, II

34. Add the following information to the file, and then create a chronological file for April 20th: VIII. April 20: 3:00 P.M. meeting between Bob Greenwood and Martin Ames. 34.____
    A. IV, V, VIII B. IV, VIII, V C. VIII, V, IV D. V, IV, VIII

35. The PRIMARY advantage of computer records over a manual system is 35.____
    A. speed of retrieval
    B. accuracy
    C. cost
    D. potential file loss

KEY (CORRECT ANSWERS)

1.	B	11.	D	21.	A	31.	C
2.	C	12.	C	22.	B	32.	D
3.	D	13.	B	23.	C	33.	B
4.	A	14.	C	24.	D	34.	A
5.	D	15.	D	25.	A	35.	A
6.	C	16.	B	26.	B		
7.	B	17.	C	27.	C		
8.	B	18.	D	28.	D		
9.	C	19.	A	29.	A		
10.	D	20.	D	30.	B		

CLERICAL ABILITIES

EXAMINATION SECTION

TEST 1

DIRECTIONS: Each question or incomplete statement is followed by several suggested answers or completions. Select the one that BEST answers the question or completes the statement. *PRINT THE LETTER OF THE CORRECT ANSWER IN THE SPACE AT THE RIGHT.*

Questions 1-4.

DIRECTIONS: Questions 1 through 4 are to be answered on the basis of the information given below.

The most commonly used filing system and the one that is easiest to learn is alphabetical filing. This involves putting records in an A to Z order, according to the letters of the alphabet. The name of a person is filed by using the following order: first, the surname or last name; second, the first name; third, the middle name or middle initial. For example, *Henry C. Young* is filed under *Y* and thereafter under *Young, Henry C.* The name of a company is filed in the same way. For example, *Long Cabinet Co.* is filed under *L* while *John T. Long Cabinet Co.* is filed under *L* and thereafter under *Long, John T. Cabinet Co.*

1. The one of the following which lists the names of persons in the CORRECT alphabetical order is: 1.____
   A. Mary Carrie, Helen Carrol, James Carson, John Carter
   B. James Carson, Mary Carrie, John Carter, Helen Carrol
   C. Helen Carrol, James Carson, John Carter, Mary Carrie
   D. John Carter, Helen Carrol, Mary Carrie, James Carson

2. The one of the following which lists the names of persons in the CORRECT alphabetical order is: 2.____
   A. Jones, John C.; Jones, John A.; Jones, John P.; Jones, John K.
   B. Jones, John P.; Jones, John K.; Jones, John C.; Jones, John A.
   C. Jones, John A.; Jones, John C.; Jones, John K.; Jones, John P.
   D. Jones, John K.; Jones, John C.; Jones, John A.; Jones, John P.

3. The one of the following which lists the names of the companies in the CORRECT alphabetical order is: 3.____
   A. Blane Co., Blake Co., Block Co., Blear Co.
   B. Blake Co., Blane Co., Blear Co., Block Co.
   C. Block Co., Blear Co., Blane Co., Blake Co.
   D. Blear Co., Blake Co., Blane Co., Block Co.

4. You are to return to the file an index card on *Barry C. Wayne Materials and Supplies Co.* 4.____
Of the following, the CORRECT alphabetical group that you should return the index card to is
A. A to G B. H to M C. N to S D. T to Z

Questions 5-10.

DIRECTIONS: In each of Questions 5 through 10, the names of four people are given. For each question, choose as your answer the one of the four names given which should be filed FIRST according to the usual system of alphabetical filing of names, as described in the following paragraph.

In filing names, you must start with the last name. Names are filed in order of the first letter of the last name, then the second letter, etc. Therefore, BAILY would be filed before BROWN, which would be filed before COLT. A name with fewer letters of the same type comes first, i.e., Smith before Smithe. If the last names are the same, the names are filed alphabetically by the first name. If the first name is an initial, a name with an initial would come before a first name that starts with the same letter as the initial. Therefore, I. BROWN would come before IRA BROWN. Finally, if both last name and first name are the same, the name would be filed alphabetically by the middle name, once again an initial coming before a middle name which starts with the same letter as the initial. If there is no middle name at all, the name would come before those with middle initials or names.

SAMPLE QUESTION: A. Lester Daniels
B. William Dancer
C. Nathan Danzig
D. Dan Lester

The last names beginning with D are filed before the last name beginning with L. Since DANIELS, DANCER, and DANZIG all begin with the same three letters, you must look at the fourth letter of the last name to determine which name should be filed first. C comes before I or Z in the alphabet, so DANCER is filed before DANIELS or DANZIG. Therefore, the answer to the above sample question is B.

5. A. Scott Biala 5.____
B. Mary Byala
C. Martin Baylor
D. Francis Bauer

6. A. Howard J. Black 6.____
B. Howard Black
C. J. Howard Black
D. John H. Black

7. A. Theodora Garth Kingston 7.____
B. Theadore Barth Kingston
C. Thomas Kingston
D. Thomas T. Kingston

8. A. Paulette Mary Huerta 8.____
   B. Paul M. Huerta
   C. Paulette L. Huerta
   D. Peter A. Huerta

9. A. Martha Hunt Morgan 9.____
   B. Martin Hunt Morgan
   C. Mary H. Morgan
   D. Martine H. Morgan

10. A. James T. Meerschaum 10.____
    B. James M. Mershum
    C. James F. Mearshaum
    D. James N. Meshum

Questions 11-14.

DIRECTIONS: Questions 11 through 14 are to be answered SOLELY on the basis of the following information.

You are required to file various documents in file drawers which are labeled according to the following pattern:

DOCUMENTS

MEMOS		LETTERS	
File	Subject	File	Subject
84PM1	(A-L)	84PC1	(A-L)
84PM2	(M-Z)	84PC2	(M-Z)

REPORTS		INQUIRIES	
File	Subject	File	Subject
84PR1	(A-L)	84PQ1	(A-L)
84PR2	(M-Z)	84PQ2	(M-Z)

11. A letter dealing with a burglary should be filed in the drawer labeled 11.____
    A. 84PM1 B. 84PC1 C. 84PR1 D. 84PQ2

12. A report on Statistics should be found in the drawer labeled 12.____
    A. 84PM1 B. 84PC2 C. 84PR2 D. 84PQS

13. An inquiry is received about parade permit procedures. It should be filed in the drawer labeled 13.____
    A. 84PM2 B. 84PC1 C. 84PR1 D. 84PQ2

14. A police officer has a question about a robbery report you filed. You should pull this file from the drawer labeled 14.____
    A. 84PM1 B. 84PM2 C. 84PR1 D. 84PR2

Questions 15-22.

DIRECTIONS: Each of Questions 15 through 22 consists of four or six numbered names. For each question, choose the option (A, B, C, or D) which indicates the order in which the names should be filed in accordance with the following filing instructions:

- File alphabetically according to last name, then first name, then middle initial.
- File according to each successive letter within a name.
- When comparing two names in which the letters in the longer name are identical to the corresponding letters in the shorter name, the shorter name is filed first.
- When the last names are the same, initials are always filed before names beginning with the same letter.

15. I. Ralph Robinson 15.____
II. Alfred Ross
III. Luis Robles
IV. James Roberts

The CORRECT filing sequence for the above names should be
A. IV, II, I, III B. I, IV, III, II C. III, IV, I, II D. IV, I, III, II

16. I. Irwin Goodwin 16.____
II. Inez Gonzalez
III. Irene Goodman
IV. Ira S. Goodwin
V. Ruth I. Goldstein
VI. M.B. Goodman

The CORRECT filing sequence for the above names should be
A. V, II, I, IV, III, VI B. V, II, VI, III, IV, I
C. V, II, III, VI, IV, I D. V, II, III, VI, I, IV

17. I. George Allan 17.____
II. Gregory Allen
III. Gary Allen
IV. George Allen

The CORRECT filing sequence for the above names should be
A. IV, III, I, II B. I, IV, II, III C. III, IV, I, II D. I, III, IV, II

18. I. Simon Kauffman 18.____
    II. Leo Kaufman
    III. Robert Kaufmann
    IV. Paul Kauffmann

    The CORRECT filing sequence for the above names should be
    A. I, IV, II, III B. II, IV, III, I C. III, II, IV, I D. I, II, III, IV

19. I. Roberta Williams 19.____
    II. Robin Wilson
    III. Roberta Wilson
    IV. Robin Williams

    The CORRECT filing sequence for the above names should be
    A. III, II, IV, I B. I, IV, III, II C. I, II, III, IV D. III, I, II, IV

20. I. Lawrence Shultz 20.____
    II. Albert Schultz
    III. Theodore Schwartz
    IV. Thomas Schwarz
    V. Alvin Schultz
    VI. Leonard Shultz

    The CORRECT filing sequence for the above names should be
    A. II, V, III, IV, I, VI B. IV, III, V, I, II, VI
    C. II, V, I, VI, III, IV D. I, VI, II, V, III, IV

21. I. McArdle 21.____
    II. Mayer
    III. Maletz
    IV. McNiff
    V. Meyer
    VI. MacMahon

    The CORRECT filing sequence for the above names should be
    A. I, IV, VI, III, II, V B. II, I, IV, VI, III, V
    C. VI, III, II, I, IV, V D. VI, III, II, V, I, IV

22. I. Jack E. Johnson 22.____
    II. R.H. Jackson
    III. Bertha Jackson
    IV. J.T. Johnson
    V. Ann Johns
    VI. John Jacobs

    The CORRECT filing sequence for the above names should be
    A. II, III, VI, V, IV, I B. III, II, VI, V, IV, I
    C. VI, II, III, I, V, IV D. III, II, VI, IV, V, I

Questions 23-30.

DIRECTIONS: The code table below shows 10 letters with matching numbers. For each question, there are three sets of letters. Each set of letters is followed by a set of numbers which may or may not match their correct letter according to the code table. For each question, check all three sets of letters and numbers and mark your answer:

A. if no pairs are correctly matched
B. if only one pair is correctly matched
C. if only two pairs are correctly matched
D. if all three pairs are correctly matched

CODE TABLE

T	M	V	D	S	P	R	G	B	H
1	2	3	4	5	6	7	8	9	0

SAMPLE QUESTION: TMVDSP – 123456
RGBHTM – 789011
DSPRGB – 256789

In the sample question above, the first set of numbers correctly match its set of letters. But the second and third pairs contain mistakes. In the second pair, M is correctly matched with number 1. According to the code table, letter M should be correctly matched with number 2. In the third pair, the letter D is incorrectly matched with number 2. According to the code table, letter D should be correctly matched with number 4. Since only one of the pairs is correctly matched, the answer to this sample question is B.

23. RSBMRM – 759262
GDSRVH – 845730
VDBRTM - 349713

23.____

24. TGVSDR – 183247
SMHRDP – 520647
TRMHSR - 172057

24.____

25. DSPRGM – 456782
MVDBHT – 234902
HPMDBT - 062491

25.____

26. BVPTRD – 936184
GDPHMB – 807029
GMRHMV - 827032

26.____

27. MGVRSH – 283750
TRDMBS – 174295
SPRMGV - 567283

27.____

28. SGBSDM – 489542 28.____
MGHPTM – 290612
MPBMHT - 269301

29. TDPBHM – 146902 29.____
VPBMRS – 369275
GDMBHM - 842902

30. MVPTBV – 236194 30.____
PDRTMB – 47128
BGTMSM - 981232

KEY (CORRECT ANSWERS)

1.	A	11.	B	21.	C
2.	C	12.	C	22.	B
3.	B	13.	D	23.	B
4.	D	14.	D	24.	B
5.	D	15.	D	25.	C
6.	B	16.	C	26.	A
7.	B	17.	D	27.	D
8.	B	18.	A	28.	A
9.	A	19.	B	29.	D
10.	C	20.	A	30.	A

TEST 2

DIRECTIONS: Each question or incomplete statement is followed by several suggested answers or completions. Select the one that BEST answers the question or completes the statement. *PRINT THE LETTER OF THE CORRECT ANSWER IN THE SPACE AT THE RIGHT.*

Questions 1-10.

DIRECTIONS: Questions 1 through 10 each consists of two columns, each containing four lines of names, numbers and/or addresses. For each question, compare the lines in Column I with the lines in Column II to see if they match exactly, and mark your answer A, B, C, or D, according to the following instructions:

A. all four lines match exactly
B. only three lines match exactly
C. only two lines match exactly
D. only one line matches exactly

		COLUMN I	COLUMN II	
1.	I.	Earl Hodgson	Earl Hodgson	1.____
	II.	1409870	1408970	
	III.	Shore Ave.	Schore Ave.	
	IV.	Macon Rd.	Macon Rd.	
2.	I.	9671485	9671485	2.____
	II.	470 Astor Court	470 Astor Court	
	III.	Halprin, Phillip	Halperin, Phillip	
	IV.	Frank D. Poliseo	Frank D. Poliseo	
3.	I.	Tandem Associates	Tandom Associates	3.____
	II.	144-17 Northern Blvd.	144-17 Northern Blvd.	
	III.	Alberta Forchi	Albert Forchi	
	IV.	Kings Park, NY 10751	Kings Point, NY 10751	
4.	I.	Bertha C. McCormack	Bertha C. McCormack	4.____
	II.	Clayton, MO	Clayton, MO	
	III.	976-4242	976-4242	
	IV.	New City, NY 10951	New City, NY 10951	
5.	I.	George C. Morill	George C. Morrill	5.____
	II.	Columbia, SC 29201	Columbia, SD 29201	
	III.	Louis Ingham	Louis Ingham	
	IV.	3406 Forest Ave.	3406 Forest Ave.	
6.	I.	506 S. Elliott Pl.	506 S. Elliott Pl.	6.____
	II.	Herbert Hall	Hurbert Hall	
	III.	4712 Rockaway Pkway	4712 Rockaway Pkway	
	IV.	169 E. 7 St.	169 E. 7 St.	

7.	I.	345 Park Ave.	345 Park Pl.	7.____
	II.	Colman Oven Corp.	Coleman Oven Corp.	
	III.	Robert Conte	Robert Conti	
	IV.	6179846	6179846	
8.	I.	Grigori Schierber	Grigori Schierber	8.____
	II.	Des Moines, Iowa	Des Moines, Iowa	
	III.	Gouverneur Hospital	Gouverneur Hospital	
	IV.	91-35 Cresskill Pl.	91-35 Cresskill Pl.	
9.	I.	Jeffery Janssen	Jeffrey Janssen	9.____
	II.	8041071	8041071	
	III.	40 Rockefeller Plaza	40 Rockafeller Plaza	
	IV.	407 6 St.	406 7 St.	
10.	I.	5971996	5871996	10.____
	II.	3113 Knickerbocker Ave.	31123 Knickerbocker Ave.	
	III.	8434 Boston Post Rd.	8424 Boston Post Rd.	
	IV.	Penn Station	Penn Station	

Questions 11-14.

DIRECTIONS: Questions 11 through 14 are to be answered by looking at the four groups of names and addresses listed below (I, II, III, and IV), and then finding out the number of groups that have their corresponding numbered lies exactly the same.

	GROUP I	GROUP II
Line 1.	Richmond General Hospital	Richman General Hospital
Line 2.	Geriatric Clinic	Geriatric Clinic
Line 3.	3975 Paerdegat St.	3975 Peardegat St.
Line 4.	Loudonville, New York 11538	Londonville, New York 11538

	GROUP III	GROUP IV
Line 1.	Richmond General Hospital	Richmend General Hospital
Line 2.	Geriatric Clinic	Geriatric Clinic
Line 3.	3795 Paerdegat St.	3975 Paerdegat St.
Line 4.	Loudonville, New York 11358	Loudonville, New York 11538

1. In how many groups is line one exactly the same? 11.____
   A. Two B. Three C. Four D. None

12. In how many groups is line two exactly the same? 12.____
   A. Two B. Three C. Four D. None

13. In how many groups is line three exactly the same? 13.____
   A. Two B. Three C. Four D. None

14. In how many groups is line four exactly the same? 14.____
    A. Two B. Three C. Four D. None

Questions 15-18.

DIRECTIONS: Each of Questions 15 through 18 has two lists of names and addresses. Each list contains three sets of names and addresses. Check each of the three sets in the list on the right to see if they are the same as the corresponding set in the list on the left. Mark your answers:
A. if none of the sets in the right list are the same as those in the left list
B. if only one of the sets in the right list is the same as those in the left list
C. if only two of the sets in the right list are the same as those in the left list
D. if all three sets in the right list are the same as those in the left list

15.	Mary T. Berlinger	Mary T. Berlinger	15.____
	2351 Hampton St.	2351 Hampton St.	
	Monsey, N.Y. 20117	Monsey, N.Y. 20117	
	Eduardo Benes	Eduardo Benes	
	483 Kingston Avenue	473 Kingston Avenue	
	Central Islip, N.Y. 11734	Central Islip, N.Y. 11734	
	Alan Carrington Fuchs	Alan Carrington Fuchs	
	17 Gnarled Hollow Road	17 Gnarled Hollow Road	
	Los Angeles, CA 91635	Los Angeles, CA 91685	
16.	David John Jacobson	David John Jacobson	16.____
	178 34 St. Apt. 4C	178 53 St. Apt. 4C	
	New York, N.Y. 00927	New York, N.Y. 00927	
	Ann-Marie Calonella	Ann-Marie Calonella	
	7243 South Ridge Blvd.	7243 South Ridge Blvd.	
	Bakersfield, CA 96714	Bakersfield, CA 96714	
	Pauline M. Thompson	Pauline M. Thomson	
	872 Linden Ave.	872 Linden Ave.	
	Houston, Texas 70321	Houston, Texas 70321	
17.	Chester LeRoy Masterton	Chester LeRoy Masterson	17.____
	152 Lacy Rd.	152 Lacy Rd.	
	Kankakee, Ill. 54532	Kankakee, Ill. 54532	
	William Maloney	William Maloney	
	S. LaCrosse Pla.	S. LaCross Pla.	
	Wausau, Wisconsin 52136	Wausau, Wisconsin 52146	
	Cynthia V. Barnes	Cynthia V. Barnes	
	16 Pines Rd.	16 Pines Rd.	
	Greenpoint, Miss. 20376	Greenpoint,, Miss. 20376	

18.	Marcel Jean Frontenac 8 Burton On The Water Calender, Me. 01471	Marcel Jean Frontenac 6 Burton On The Water Calender, Me. 01471	18.____
	J. Scott Marsden 174 S. Tipton St. Cleveland, Ohio	J. Scott Marsden 174 Tipton St. Cleveland, Ohio	
	Lawrence T. Haney 171 McDonough St. Decatur, Ga. 31304	Lawrence T. Haney 171 McDonough St. Decatur, Ga. 31304	

Questions 19-26.

DIRECTIONS: Each of Questions 19 through 26 has two lists of numbers. Each list contains three sets of numbers. Check each of the three sets in the list on the right to see if they are the same as the corresponding set in the list on the left. Mark your answers:

A. if none of the sets in the right list are the same as those in the left list
B. if only one of the sets in the right list is the same as those in the left list
C. if only two of the sets in the right list are the same as those in the left list
D. if all three sets in the right list are the same as those in the left lists

19.	7354183476 4474747744 5791430231	7354983476 4474747774 57914302311	19.____
20.	7143592185 8344517699 9178531263	7143892185 8344518699 9178531263	20.____
21.	2572114731 8806835476 8255831246	257214731 8806835476 8255831246	21.____
22.	331476853821 6976658532996 3766042113715	331476858621 6976655832996 3766042113745	22.____
23.	8806663315 74477138449 211756663666	88066633115 74477138449 211756663666	23.____

24. 990006966996 | 99000696996 | 24.____
53022219743 | 53022219843
4171171117717 | 4171171177717

25. 24400222433004 | 24400222433004 | 25.____
5300030055000355 | 5300030055500355
2000075532002022 | 2000075532002022

26. 611166640660001116 | 61116664066001116 | 26.____
7111300117001100733 | 7111300117001100733
26666446664476518 | 26666446664476518

Questions 27-30.

DIRECTIONS: Questions 27 through 30 are to be answered by picking the answer which is in the correct numerical order, from the lowest number to the highest number, in each question.

27. A. 44533, 44518, 44516, 44547 27.____
B. 44516, 44518, 44533, 44547
C. 44547, 44533, 44518, 44516
D. 44518, 44516, 44547, 44533

28. A. 95587, 95593, 95601, 95620 28.____
B. 95601, 95620, 95587, 95593
C. 95593, 95587, 95601. 95620
D. 95620, 95601, 95593, 95587

29. A. 232212, 232208, 232232, 232223 29.____
B. 232208, 232223, 232212, 232232
C. 232208, 232212, 232223, 232232
D. 232223, 232232, 232208, 232208

30. A. 113419, 113521, 113462, 113462 30.____
B. 113588, 113462, 113521, 113419
C. 113521, 113588, 113419, 113462
D. 113419, 113462, 113521, 113588

KEY (CORRECT ANSWERS)

1.	C	11.	A	21.	C
2.	B	12.	C	22.	A
3.	D	13.	A	23.	D
4.	A	14.	A	24.	A
5.	C	15.	C	25.	C
6.	B	16.	B	26.	C
7.	D	17.	B	27.	B
8.	A	18.	B	28.	A
9.	D	19.	B	29.	C
10.	C	20.	B	30.	D

NAME AND NUMBER CHECKING

EXAMINATION SECTION

TEST 1

DIRECTIONS: This test is designed to measure your speed/and accuracy. You are urged to work both quickly and accurately and to do correctly as many lists as you can in the time allowed. The test consists of lists or pairs of names and numbers. Count the number of IDENTICAL pairs in each list. Then, select the correct number, 1, 2, 3, 4, 5, and indicate your choice in the space at the right. Two sample questions are presented for your guidance, together with the correct solutions.

SAMPLE LIST A
Adelphi College – Adelphia College
Braxton Corp – Braxeton Corp.
Wassaic State School – Wassaic State School
Central Islip State Hospital – Central Isllip State Hospital
Greenwich House – Greenwich House

NOTE: There are only two correct pairs—Wassaic State School and Greenwich House. Therefore, the CORRECT answer is 2.

SAMPLE LIST B
78453694 – 78453684
784530 – 784530
533 – 534
67845 – 67845
2368745 – 2368755

NOTE: There are only two correct pairs—784530 and 67845. Therefore, the CORRECT answer is 2.

LIST 1 1.____
Diagnostic Clinic – Diagnostic Clinic
Yorkville Health – Yorkville Health
Meinhard Clinic – Meinhart Clinic
Corlears Clinic – Carlears Clinic
Tremont Diagnostic – Tremont Diagnostic

LIST 2 2.____
73526 – 73526
7283627198 – 7283627198
627 – 637
728352617283 – 7283526178282
6281 – 6281

LIST 3		3.____
Jefferson Clinic	– Jeffersen Clinic	
Mott Haven Center	– Mott Havan Center	
Bronx Hospital	– Bronx Hospital	
Montefiore Hospital	– Montifeore Hospital	
Beth Isreal Hospital	– Beth Israel Hospital	
LIST 4		4.____
936271826	– 936371826	
5271	– 5291	
82637192037	– 82637192037	
527182	– 5271882	
726354256	- 72635456	
LIST 5		5.____
Trinity Hospital	– Trinity Hospital	
Central Harlem	– Centrel Harlem	
St. Luke's Hospital	– St. Lukes' Hospital	
Mt. Sinai Hospital	– Mt. Sinia Hospital	
N.Y. Dispensery	– N.Y. Dispensary	
LIST 6		6.____
725361552637	– 725361555637	
7526378	– 7526377	
6975	– 6975	
82637481028	– 82637481028	
3427	– 3429	
LIST 7		7.____
Misericordia Hospital	– Miseracordia Hospital	
Lebonan Hospital	– Lebanon Hospital	
Gouverneur Hospital	– Gouverner Hospital	
German Polyclinic	– German Policlinic	
French Hospital	– French Hospital	
LIST 8		8.____
8277364933251	– 827364933351	
63728	– 63728	
367281	– 367281	
62733846273	– 6273846293	
62836	- 6283	
LIST 9		9.____
King's County Hospital	– Kings County Hospital	
St. Johns Long Island	– St. John's Long Island	
Bellevue Hospital	– Bellvue Hospital	
Beth David Hospital	– Beth David Hospital	
Samaritan Hospital	– Samariton Hospital	

LIST 10		10.____
62836454	– 62836455	
42738267	– 42738369	
573829	– 573829	
738291627874	– 738291627874	
725	- 735	
LIST 11		11.____
Bloomingdal Clinic	– Bloomingdale Clinic	
Communitty Hospital	– Community Hospital	
Metroplitan Hospital	– Metropoliton Hospital	
Lenox Hill Hospital	– Lonex Hill Hospital	
Lincoln Hospital	– Lincoln Hospital	
LIST 12		12.____
6283364728	– 6283648	
627385	– 627383	
54283902	– 54283602	
63354	– 63354	
7283562781	- 7283562781	
LIST 13		13.____
Sydenham Hospital	– Sydanham Hospital	
Roosevalt Hospital	– Roosevelt Hospital	
Vanderbilt Clinic	– Vanderbild Clinic	
Women's Hospital	– Woman's Hospital	
Flushing Hospital	– Flushing Hospital	
LIST 14		14.____
62738	– 62738	
727355542321	– 72735542321	
263849332	– 263849332	
262837	– 263837	
47382912	- 47382922	
LIST 15		15.____
Episcopal Hospital	– Episcapal Hospital	
Flower Hospital	– Flouer Hospital	
Stuyvesent Clinic	– Stuyvesant Clinic	
Jamaica Clinic	– Jamaica Clinic	
Ridgwood Clinic	– Ridgewood Clinic	
LIST 16		16.____
628367299	– 628367399	
111	– 111	
118293304829	– 1182839489	
4448	– 4448	
333693678	- 333693678	

LIST 17		17.____
Arietta Crane Farm	– Areitta Crane Farm	
Bikur Chilim Home	– Bikur Chilom Home	
Burke Foundation	– Burke Foundation	
Blythedale Home	– Blythdale Home	
Campbell Cottages	– Cambell Cottages	
LIST 18		18.____
32123	– 32132	
273893326783	– 27389326783	
473829	– 473829	
7382937	– 7383937	
3628890122332	- 36289012332	
LIST 19		19.____
Caraline Rest	– Caroline Rest	
Loreto Rest	– Loretto Rest	
Edgewater Creche	– Edgwater Creche	
Holiday Farm	– Holiday Farm	
House of St. Giles	– House of st. Giles	
LIST 20		20.____
557286777	– 55728677	
3678902	– 3678892	
1567839	– 1567839	
7865434712	– 7865344712	
9927382	- 9927382	
LIST 21		21.____
Isabella Home	– Isabela Home	
James A. Moore Home	– James A. More Home	
The Robin's Nest	– The Roben's Nest	
Pelham Home	– Pelam Home	
St. Eleanora's Home	– St. Eleanora's Home	
LIST 22		22.____
273648293048	– 273648293048	
334	– 334	
7362536478	– 7362536478	
7362819273	– 7362819273	
7362	- 7363	
LIST 23		23.____
St. Pheobe's Mission	– St. Phebe's Mission	
Seaside Home	– Seaside Home	
Speedwell Society	– Speedwell Society	
Valeria Home	– Valera Home	
Wiltwyck	- Wildwyck	

LIST 24 24.____

63728	– 63738
63728192736	– 63728192738
428	– 458
62738291527	– 62738291529
63728192	- 63728192

LIST 25 25.____

McGaffin	– McGafin
David Ardslee	– David Ardslee
Axton Supply	– Axeton Supply Co
Alice Russell	– Alice Russell
Dobson Mfg. Co.	– Dobsen Mfg. Co.

KEY (CORRECT ANSWERS)

1.	3	11.	1
2.	3	12.	2
3.	1	13.	1
4.	1	14.	2
5.	1	15.	1
6.	2	16.	3
7.	1	17.	1
8.	2	18.	1
9.	1	19.	1
10.	2	20.	2

21.	1
22.	4
23.	2
24.	1
25.	2

TEST 2

DIRECTIONS: This test is designed to measure your speed/and accuracy. You are urged to work both quickly and accurately and to do correctly as many lists as you can in the time allowed. The test consists of lists or pairs of names and numbers. Count the number of IDENTICAL pairs in each list. Then, select the correct number, 1, 2, 3, 4, 5, and indicate your choice in the space at the right.

LIST 1 1.____

82637381028 – 82637281028
928 – 928
72937281028 – 72937281028
7362 – 7362
927382615 – 927382615

LIST 2 2.____

Albee Theatre – Albee Theatre
Lapland Lumber Co. – Laplund Lumber Co.
Adelphi College – Adelphi College
Jones & Son Inc. – Jones & Sons Inc.
S.W. Ponds Co. – S.W. Ponds Co.

LIST 3 3.____

85345 – 85345
895643278 – 895643277
726352 – 726353
632685 – 632685
7263524 – 7236524

LIST 4 4.____

Eagle Library – Eagle Library
Dodge Ltd. – Dodge Co.
Stromberg Carlson – Stromberg Carlsen
Clairice Ling – Clairice Linng
Mason Book Co. – Matson Book Co.

LIST 5 5.____

66273 – 66273
629 – 629
7382517283 – 7382517283
637281 – 639281
2738261 – 2788261

LIST 6 6.____

Robert MacColl – Robert McColl
Buick Motor – Buck Motors
Murray Bay & Co. Ltd. – Murray Bay Co. Ltd.
L.T. Ltyle – L.T. Lyttle
A.S. Landas – A.S. Landas

LIST 7		7.____
6271526374890	– 627152637490	
73526189	– 73526189	
5372	– 5392	
637281142	– 63728124	
4783946	– 4783046	
LIST 8		8.____
Tyndall Burke	– Tyndell Burke	
W. Briehl	– W. Briehl	
Burritt Publishing Co.	– Buritt Publishing Co.	
Frederick Breyer & Co.	– Frederick Breyer Co.	
Bailey Buulard	– Bailey Bullard	
LIST 9		9.____
634	– 634	
16837	– 163837	
273892223678	– 27389223678	
527182	– 527782	
3628901223	– 3629002223	
LIST 10		10.____
Ernest Boas	– Ernest Boas	
Rankin Barne	– Rankin Barnes	
Edward Appley	– Edward Appely	
Camel	– Camel	
Caiger Food Co.	– Caiger Food Co.	
LIST 11		11.____
6273	– 6273	
322	– 332	
15672839	– 15672839	
63728192637	– 63728192639	
738	– 738	
LIST 12		12.____
Wells Fargo Co.	– Wells Fargo Co.	
W.D. Brett	– W.D. Britt	
Tassco Co.	– Tassko Co.	
Republic Mills	– Republic Mill	
R.W. Burnham	– R.W. Burhnam	
LIST 13		13.____
7253529152	– 7283529152	
6283	– 6383	
52839102738	– 5283910238	
308	– 398	
82637201927	– 8263720127	

LIST 14		14.____
Schumacker Co.	– Shumacker Co.	
C.H. Caiger	– C.H. Caiger	
Abraham Strauss	– Abram Straus	
B.F. Boettjer	– B.F. Boettijer	
Cut-Rate Store	– Cut-Rate Stores	
LIST 15		15.____
15273826	– 15273826	
72537	– 73537	
726391027384	– 62639107384	
637389	– 627399	
725382910	– 725382910	
LIST 16		16.____
Hixby Ltd.	– Hixby Lt'd.	
S. Reiner	– S. Riener	
Reynard Co.	– Reynord Co.	
Esso Gassoline Co.	– Esso Gasolene Co.	
Belle Brock	– Belle Brock	
LIST 17		17.____
7245	– 7245	
819263728192	– 819263728172	
682537289	– 682537298	
789	– 789	
82936542891	– 82936542891	
LIST 18		18.____
Joseph Cartwright	– Joseph Cartwrite	
Foote Food Co.	– Foot Food Co.	
Weiman & Held	– Weiman & Held	
Sanderson Shoe Co.	– Sandersen Shoe Co.	
A.M. Byrne	– A.N. Byrne	
LIST 19		19.____
4738267	– 4738277	
63728	– 63729	
6283628901	– 6283628991	
918264	– 918264	
263728192037	– 2637728192073	
LIST 20		20.____
Exray Laboratories	– Exray Labratories	
Curley Toy Co.	– Curly Toy Co.	
J. Lauer & Cross	– J. Laeur & Cross	
Mireco Brands	– Mireco Brands	
Sandor Lorand	– Sandor Larand	

LIST 21		21.____
607	– 609	
6405	– 6403	
976	– 996	
101267	– 101267	
2065432	– 20965432	
LIST 22		22.____
John Macy & Sons	– John Macy & Son	
Venus Pencil Co.	– Venus Pencil Co.	
Nell McGinnis	– Nell McGinnis	
McCutcheon & Co.	– McCutcheon & Co.	
Sun-Tan Oil	– Sun-Tan Oil	
LIST 23		23.____
703345700	– 703345700	
46754	– 466754	
3367490	– 3367490	
3379	– 3778	
47384	– 47394	
LIST 24		24.____
arthritis	– arthritis	
asthma	– asthma	
endocrine	– endocrene	
gastro-enterological	– gastrol-enteralogical	
orthopedic	– orthopedic	
LIST 25		25.____
743829432	– 743828432	
998	– 998	
732816253902	– 732816252902	
46829	– 46830	
7439120249	– 7439210249	

KEY (CORRECT ANSWERS)

1. 4
2. 3
3. 2
4. 1
5. 2

6. 1
7. 2
8. 1
9. 1
10. 3

11. 3
12. 1
13. 1
14. 1
15. 2

16. 1
17. 3
18. 1
19. 1
20. 1

21. 1
22. 4
23. 2
24. 3
25. 1

NUMBER COMPARISONS

EXAMINATION SECTION

TEST 1

DIRECTIONS: This test consists of 200 questions in which pairs of numbers are to be examined for exactness. If the two numbers are exactly the same, mark the answer "A" on the line provided between the two. If they are different, mark the answer "B". This is a test for speed and accuracy. Work as fast as you can without making mistakes.

1.	307	_______	309
2.	4605	_______	4603
3.	976	_______	979
4.	101267	_______	101267
5.	3065432	_______	30965432
6.	103345700	_______	103345700
7.	46754	_______	466754
8.	3367490	_______	3367490
9.	2779	_______	2778
10.	57394	_______	57394
11.	63801829374	_______	63801839474
12.	283577657	_______	283577657
13.	75689	_______	75689
14.	2547892026	_______	2547893026
15.	336354	_______	336254
16.	998745732	_______	998745733
17.	623	_______	623
18.	263849102983	_______	263849102983
19.	5870	_______	5870
20.	379012	_______	379012
21.	8734629	_______	8734629
22.	2549806746	_______	2549806746
23.	57802564	_______	57892564
24.	689246	_______	688246
25.	1578024683	_______	1578024683
26.	582039485618	_______	582039485618
27.	63829172630	_______	63829172639
28.	592	_______	592
29.	829374820	_______	829374820
30.	62937456	_______	63937456

31.	8293	________	8293
32.	6382910293	________	6382910292
33.	781928374012	________	781928374912
34.	68293	________	38393
35.	18203649271	________	18293649271
36.	4820384	________	4820384
37.	283019283745	________	283019283745
38.	73927102	________	73927102
39.	91029354829	________	91029354829
40.	38291728	________	38291728
41.	6283910293	________	6283910203
42.	392018273648	________	392018273848
43.	820	________	829
44.	572937273	________	572937373
45.	7392	________	7392
46.	8172036	________	8172036
47.	68391028364	________	68391028394
48.	48293	________	48292
49.	739201	________	739201
50.	62839201	________	62839211
51.	5829	________	5820
52.	192836472829	________	192836472829
53.	362	________	362
54.	2039271827	________	2039276837
55.	73829	________	73829
56.	82739102837	________	82739102837
57.	48891028	________	48891028
58.	7291728	________	7291928
59.	172839102839	________	172839102839
60.	628192	________	628102
61.	473829432	________	473829432
62.	478	________	478
63.	372816253902	________	372816252902
64.	64829	________	64830
65.	4739210249	________	4739210249
66.	748362	________	748363
67.	728354792	________	728354772
68.	3927	________	3927
69.	927384625	________	927384625
70.	4628156	________	4628158

71.	6382	________	6392
72.	12937453829	________	12937453829
73.	523	________	533
74.	7263920	________	7163920
75.	74293	________	74293
76.	82734291	________	82734271
77.	2739102637	________	2739102637
78.	62810263849	________	62810263846
79.	638291	________	638291
80.	62831027	________	62831027
81.	527	________	529
82.	172438291026	________	172438291026
83.	7253829142	________	725382942
84.	836287	________	836289
85.	62435162839	________	62435162839
86.	6254	________	6256
87.	6241526	________	6241526
88.	1426389012	________	1426389102
89.	825	________	825
90.	67253917287	________	67253917287
91.	6271	________	6271
92.	263819253627	________	263819253629
93.	82637	________	82937
94.	728392736	________	728392736
95.	62739	________	32739
96.	728352689	________	728352688
97.	463728	________	463728
98.	73829176	________	73827196
99.	4825367	________	4825369
100.	56382018	________	56382018
101.	789	________	789
102.	819263728192	________	819263728172
103.	682537289	________	682537298
104.	7245	________	7245
105.	82936542891	________	82936542891
106.	4738267	________	4737277
107.	63728	________	63729
108.	6283628901	________	6283628991
109.	918264	________	918264
110.	263728192037	________	263728192073

4 (#1)

111.	528391025283910238	________	52839102738
112.	6283	________	6182
113.	7283529152	________	7283529152
114.	208	________	298
115.	82637201927	________	8263720127
116.	15273826	________	15273826
117.	72537	________	73537
118.	726391027384	________	726391027384
119.	627389	________	627399
120	7253829910	________	725382910
121.	46273	________	46273
122.	629	________	620
123.	7382517283	________	7382517283
124.	637281	________	528281
125.	2738261	________	2728261
126.	627152637490	________	627152637490
127.	73526189	________	73526189
128.	5372	________	5392
129.	63728142	________	63728142
130.	4783946	________	4783046
131.	826372810428	________	82637281028
132.	628	________	628
133.	7293728172	________	7293728177
134.	7362	________	7362
135.	927382615	________	927382615
136.	84345	________	85345
137.	894643278	________	895642377
138.	726352	________	726353
139.	7263524	________	7263524
140.	632685	________	632685
141.	273648293048	________	273648293048
142.	634	________	634
143.	7362536478	________	7362536478
144.	7362	________	7363
145.	7362819273	________	7362819273
146.	63728	________	63738
147	63728192637	________	63728192639
148.	728	________	738
149.	62738291527	________	62738291529
150.	63728192	________	63728192

151.	73526	________	73525
152.	728367189	________	7283627189
153.	627	________	637
154.	728352617283	________	7283526617282
155.	6281	________	6381
156.	936271826	________	936371826
157.	82637192037	________	72636192936
158.	527182	________	527182
159.	6273	________	6273
160.	726354256	________	72635456
161.	725361552637	________	725361555637
162.	7526378	________	7526377
163.	685	________	685
164.	82637481028	________	82637481028
165.	3427	________	3429
166.	82736493351	________	82736493351
167.	63728	________	63728
168.	6273846273	________	6273846293
169.	62836	________	6283
170.	2638496	________	2637496
171.	738291627874	________	738291627874
172.	62826454	________	62836455
173.	42738267	________	42738269
174.	573929	________	573829
175.	628364728	________	628364928
176.	725	________	735
177.	627385	________	627383
178.	63354	________	63354
179	54283902	________	54283602
180	7283562781	________	7283562781
181.	62738	________	63738
182.	72735542321	________	72735542321
183.	263849332	________	263849332
184.	162837	________	163837
185.	47382912	________	47382922

6 (#1)

186.	628367299	________	628367399
187.	111	________	111
188.	11829304829	________	11828304829
189.	4448	________	4448
190.	333693678	________	333693678
191.	3212	________	3212
192.	27389223678	________	27389223678
193.	473829	________	473829
194.	7382937	________	7383937
195.	3628901223	________	3628901233
196.	5572867	________	5572867
197.	87263543	________	87263543
198.	3678902	________	3678892
199.	15672839	________	15672839
200.	9927382	________	9927382

KEY (CORRECT ANSWERS)

1.	B	41.	B	81.	B	121.	A	161.	B
2.	B	42.	B	82.	A	122.	B	162.	B
3.	B	43.	B	83.	B	123.	A	163.	A
4.	A	44.	B	84.	B	124.	B	164.	A
5.	B	45.	A	85.	A	125.	B	165.	B
6.	A	46.	A	86.	B	126.	A	166.	B
7.	B	47.	B	87.	A	127.	A	167	A
8.	A	48.	B	88.	B	128.	B	168.	B
9.	B	49.	A	89.	A	129.	B	169.	B
10.	A	50.	B	90.	A	130.	B	170.	A
11.	B	51.	B	91.	A	131.	A	171.	A
12.	A	52.	A	92.	B	132.	A	172.	B
13.	A	53.	A	93.	B	133.	B	173.	B
14.	B	54.	B	94.	A	134.	A	174.	A
15.	B	55.	A	95.	A	135.	A	175.	B
16.	B	56.	A	96.	B	136.	A	176.	B
17.	A	57.	A	97.	A	137.	B	177.	B
18.	A	58.	B	98.	B	138.	B	178.	A
19.	A	59.	A	99.	B	139.	A	179.	B
20.	A	60.	B	100.	A	140.	A	180.	A
21.	A	61.	A	101.	A	141.	A	181.	B
22.	A	62.	A	102.	B	142.	A	182.	B
23.	B	63.	A	103.	B	143.	A	183.	A
24.	B	64.	B	104.	A	144.	B	184.	B
25.	A	65.	A	105.	A	145.	A	185.	B
26.	A	66.	B	106.	B	146.	B	186.	B
27.	B	67.	B	107.	B	147.	B	187.	A
28.	A	68.	A	108.	B	148.	B	188.	B
29.	A	69.	A	109.	A	149.	B	189.	A
30.	B	70.	B	110.	B	150.	B	190.	A
31.	A	71.	B	111.	B	151.	A	191.	A
32.	B	72.	A	112.	B	152.	A	192.	A
33.	B	73.	B	113.	A	153.	B	193.	A
34.	B	74.	A	114.	B	154.	B	194.	B
35.	B	75.	A	115.	B	155.	B	195.	B
36.	A	76.	B	116.	A	156.	A	196.	A
37.	A	77.	A	117.	B	157.	A	197.	A
38.	A	78.	B	118.	A	158.	A	198.	B
39.	A	79.	A	119.	B	159.	A	199.	A
40.	A	80.	A	120.	A	160.	B	200.	A

ARITHMETICAL REASONING

EXAMINATION SECTION

TEST 1

DIRECTIONS: Each question or incomplete statement is followed by several suggested answers or completions. Select the one that BEST answers the question or completes the statement. *PRINT THE LETTER OF THE CORRECT ANSWER IN THE SPACE AT THE RIGHT.*

1. The ABC Corporation had a gross income of $125,500.00 in 2019. Of this, it paid 60% for overhead. 1.____
   If the gross income for 2020 increased by $6,500 and the cost of overhead increased to 61% of gross income, how much MORE did it pay for overhead in 2020 than in 2019?
   A. $1,320 B. $5,220 C. $7,530 D. $8,052

2. After one year, Mr. Richards paid back a total of $16,950 as payment for a $15,000 loan. All the money paid over $15,000 was simple interest. 2.____
   The interest charge was MOST NEARLY
   A. 13% B. 11% C. 9% D. 7%

3. A checking account has a balance of $253.36. 3.____
   If deposits of $36.95, $210.23, and $7.34 and withdrawals of $117.35, $23.37, and $15.98 are made, what is the NEW balance of the account?
   A. $155.54 B. $351.18 C. $364.58 D. $664.58

4. In 2020, the W Realty Company spent 27% of its income on rent. 4.____
   If it earned $97,254 in 2020, the amount it paid for rent was
   A. $26,258.58 B. 26,348.58 C. $27,248.58 D. $27,358.58

5. Six percent simple annual interest on $2,436.18 is MOST NEARLY 5.____
   A. $145.08 B. $145.17 C. $146.08 D. $146.17

6. H. Partridge receives a weekly gross salary (before deductions) of $397.50. Through weekly payroll deductions of $13.18, he is paying back a loan he took from his pension fund. 6.____
   If other fixed weekly deductions amount to $122.76, how much pay would Mr. Partridge take home over a period of 33 weeks?
   A. $7,631.28 B. $8,250.46 C. $8,631.48 D. $13,117.50

7. Mr. Robertson is a city employee enrolled in a city retirement system. He has taken out a loan from the retirement fund and is paying it back at the rate of $14.90 every two weeks. 7.____
   In eighteen weeks, how much money will he have paid back on the loan?
   A. $268.20 B. $152.80 C. $134.10 D. $67.05

8. In 2019, The Iridor Book Company had the following expenses: rent, $6,500; overhead, $52,585; inventory, $35,700; and miscellaneous, $1,275. If all of these expenses went up 18% in 2020, what would they TOTAL in 2020? 8.____
   A. $17,290.80 B. $78,769.20 C. $96,060.00 D. $113,350.80

9. Ms. Ranier had a gross salary of $710.72 paid once every two weeks. If the deductions from each paycheck are $125.44, $50.26, $12.58, and $2.54, how much money would Ms. Ranier take home in eight weeks? 9.____
   A. $2,079.60 B. $2,842.88 C. $4,159.20 D. $5,685.76

10. Mr. Martin had a net income of $95,500 in 2019. If he spent 34% on rent and household expenses, 3% on house furnishings, 25% on clothes, and 36% on food, how much was left for savings and other expenses? 10.____
   A. $980 B. $1,910 C. $3,247 D. $9,800

11. Mr. Elsberg can pay back a loan of $1,800 from the city employees' retirement system if he pays back $36.69 every two weeks for two full years. At the end of the two years, how much more than the original $1,800 he borrowed will Mr. Elsberg have paid back? 11.____
   A. $53.94 B. $107.88 C. $190.79 D. $214.76

12. Mr. Nusbaum is a city employee receiving a gross salary (salary before deductions) of $20,800. Every two weeks, the following deductions are taken out of his salary: Federal Income Tax, $162.84; FICA, $44.26; State Tax, $29.2; City Tax, $13.94; Health Insurance, $3.14. If Mr. Nusbaum's salary and deductions remained the same for a full calendar year, what would his net salary (gross salary less deductions) be in that year? 12.____
   A. $6,596.20 B. $14,198.60 C. $18,745.50 D. $20,546.30

13. Add: 8936, 7821, 8953, 4297, 9785, 6579. 13.____
   A. 45,371 B. 45,381 C. 46,371 D. 46,381

14. Multiply: 987 × 867 14.____
   A. 854,609 B. 854,729 C. 855,709 D. 855,729

15. Divide: $59\overline{)321439.0}$ 15.____
   A. 5438.1 B. 5447.1 C. 5448.1 D. 5457.1

16. Divide: $.052\overline{)721}$ 16.____
   A. 12,648.0 B. 12,648.1 C. 12,649.0 D. 12,649.1

17. If the total number of employees in one city agency increased from 1,927 to 2,006 during a certain year, the percentage increase in the number of employees for that year is MOST NEARLY 17.____
   A. 4% B. 5% C. 6% D. 7%

18. During a single fiscal year, which totaled 248 workdays, one account clerk verified 1,488 purchase vouchers. 18.____
Assuming a normal work week of five days, what is the AVERAGE number of vouchers verified by the account clerk in a one-week period during this fiscal year?
A. 25 B. 30 C. 35 D. 40

19. Multiplying a number by .75 is the same as 19.____
A. multiplying it by $^2/_3$ B. dividing it by $^2/_3$
C. multiplying it by ¾ D. dividing it by ¾

20. In City Agency A, $^2/_3$ of the employees are enrolled in a retirement system. City Agency B has the same number of employees as Agency A and 60% of these are enrolled in a retirement system. 20.____
If Agency A has a total of 660 employees, how many MORE employees does it have enrolled in a retirement system than does Agency B?
A. 36 B. 44 C. 56 D. 66

21. Net worth is equal to assets minus liabilities. 21.____
If, at the end of 2019, a textile company had assets of $98,695.83 and liabilities of $59,238.29, what was its net worth?
A. $38,478.54 B. $38,488.64 C. $39,457.54 D. $48,557.54

22. Mr. Martin's assets consist of the following: Cash on hand, $5,233.74, Automobile, $3,206.09; Furniture, $4,925.00; Government Bonds, $5,500.00; and House, $36,69.85. 22.____
What are his TOTAL assets?
A. $54,545.68 B. $54,455.68 C. $55,455.68 D. $55,555.68

23. If Mr. Mitchell has $627.04 in his checking account and then writes three checks for $241.75, $13.24, and $102.97, what will be his new balance? 23.____
A. $257.88 B. $269.08 C. $357.96 D. $369.96

24. An employee's net pay is equal to his total earnings less all deductions. 24.____
If an employee's total earnings in a pay period are $497.05, what is his net pay if he has the following deductions: Federal Income Tax, $18.79; City Tax, $7.25; Pension, $1.88?
A. $351.17 B. $351.07 C. $350.17 D. $350.07

25. A petty cash fund had an opening balance of $85.75 on December 1. Expenditures of $23.00, $15.65, $5.23, $14.75, and $26.38 were made out of this fund during the first 14 days of the month. Then, on December 17, another $38.50 was added to the fund. 25.____
If additional expenditures of $17.18, $3.29, and $11.64 were made during the remainder of the month, what was the FINAL balance of the petty cash fund at the end of December?
A. $6.93 B. $7.13 C. $46.51 D. $91.40

KEY (CORRECT ANSWERS)

1.	B	11.	B
2.	A	12.	B
3.	B	13.	C
4.	A	14.	D
5.	D	15.	C
6.	C	16.	D
7.	C	17.	A
8.	D	18.	B
9.	A	19.	C
10.	B	20.	B

21.	C
22.	D
23.	B
24.	D
25.	B

SOLUTIONS TO PROBLEMS

1. (\$132,000)(.61) – (\$125,500)(.60) = \$5,220

2. Interest = \$1,950. As a percent, \$1950 ÷ 15,000 = 13%

3. New balance = \$253.36 + \$36.95 + \$210.23 + \$7.34 - \$117.35 - \$23.37 - \$15.98 = \$351.18

4. Rent = (\$97,254)(.27) = \$26,258.58

5. (\$2,436.18)(.06) ≈ \$146.17

6. (\$397.50 - \$13.18 - \$122.76) = \$8,631.48

7. (\$14.90)($\frac{18}{2}$) = \$134.10

8. (\$6,500 + \$52,585 + \$35,700 + \$1,275)(1.18) = \$113,350.80

9. (\$710.72 - \$125.44 - \$50.26 - \$12.58 - \$2.54)($\frac{8}{2}$) = \$2,079.60

10. (1 - .34 - .03 - .25 - .36) - \$1,800 = \$107.88

11. (36.69)(52) - \$1,800 = \$107.88

12. \$20,800 – (26)(\$162.84+\$44.26+\$29.72+\$13.94+\$3.14) = \$14,198.60

13. 8,936 + 7,821 + 8,953 + 4,297 + 9,785 + 6,579 = 46,371

14. (987)(867) – 855,729

15. 321,439 ÷ 59 ≈ 5,448.1

16. 721 ÷ .057 ≈ 12,649.1

17. (2,006-1,927) ÷ 1,927 ≈ 4%

18. Let x = number of vouchers. Then, $\frac{x}{5} = \frac{1488}{248}$. Solving, x = 30

19. Multiplying by .75 is equivalent to multiplying by $\frac{3}{4}$

20. (660)($\frac{2}{3}$) – (660)(.60) = 44

21. Net worth = \$98,695.83 - \$59,238.29 = \$39,457.54

22. Total Assets = \$5,233.74 + \$3,206.09 + \$4,925.00 + \$5,500.00) + \$36,690.85 = \$55,555.68.

23. New balance = \$627.04 - \$241.75 - \$13.24 - \$102.97 = \$269.08

24. Net pay = \$497.05 - \$90.32 - \$28.74 - \$18.79 - \$7.25 - \$1.88 = \$350.07

25. Final balance = \$85.75 - \$23.00 - \$15.65 - \$5.23 - \$14.75 - \$26.38 + \$38.50 - \$17.18 - \$3.29 - \$11.64 = \$7.13

TEST 2

DIRECTIONS: Each question or incomplete statement is followed by several suggested answers or completions. Select the one that BEST answers the question or completes the statement. *PRINT THE LETTER OF THE CORRECT ANSWER IN THE SPACE AT THE RIGHT.*

1. The formula for computing base salary is: Earnings equals base gross plus additional gross. 1.____
If an employee's earnings during a particular period are in the amounts of $597.45, $535.92, $639.91, and $552.83, and his base gross salary is $525.50 per paycheck, what is the TOTAL of the additional gross earned by the employee during that period?
A. $224.11 B. $224.21 C. $224.51 D. $244.11

2. If a lump sum death benefit is paid by the retirement system in an amount equal to 3/7 of an employee's last yearly salary of $13,486.50, the amount of the death benefit paid is MOST NEARLY 2.____
A. $5,749.29 B. $5,759.92 C. $5,779.92 D. $5,977.29

3. Suppose that a member has paid 15 installments on a 28-installment loan. The percentage of the number of installments paid to the retirement system is 3.____
A. 53.57% B. 53.97% C. 54.57% D. 55.37%

4. If an employee takes a 1-month vacation during a calendar year, the percentage of the year during which he works is MOST NEARLY 4.____
A. 90.9% B. 91.3% C. 91.6% D. 92.1%

5. Suppose that an employee took a leave of absence totaling 7 months during a calendar year. 5.____
Assuming the employee did not take any vacation time during the remainder of that year, the percentage of the year in which he worked is MOST NEARLY
A. 41.7% B. 43.3% C. 46.5% D. 47.1%

6. A member has borrowed $4,725 from her funds in the retirement system. 6.____
If $3,213 has been repaid, the percentage of the loan which is still outstanding is MOST NEARLY
A. 16% B. 32% C. 48% D. 68%

7. If an employee worked only 24 weeks during the year because of illness, the portion of the year he was out of work was MOST NEARLY 7.____
A. 46% B. 48% C. 51% D. 54%

8. If an employee purchased credit for a 16-week period of service which he had prior to rejoining the retirement system, the percentage of a year he purchased credit for was MOST NEARLY 8.____
A. 27.9% B. 28.8% C. 30.7% D. 33.3%

9. If an employee contributes 2/11 of his yearly salary to his pension fund account, the percentage of his yearly salary which he contributes is MOST NEARLY 9.____
A. 17.9% B. 18.2% C. 18.4% D. 19.0%

10. In 2018, the maximum amount of income from which social security tax could be withheld (base salary) was $70,500. In 2020, the base salary was $82,500. The 2020 base salary represents a percentage increase over the 2018 base salary of APPROXIMATELY 10.____
A. 15% B. 16% C. 17% D. 18%

11. If 17.5% of an employee's salary is withheld for taxes, the one of the following which is the fraction of the salary withheld is 11.____
A. 3/20 B. 8/35 C. 7/40 D. 4/25

12. If a person withdraws 42% of the funds from his account with the retirement system, the remaining balance represents a fraction of MOST NEARLY 12.____
A. 7/13 B. 5/9 C. 7/12 D. 4/7

13. A property decreases in value from $45,000 to $35,000. The percent of decrease is MOST NEARLY 13.____
A. 20.5% B. 22.2% C. 25.0% D. 28.6%

14. The fraction $\frac{487}{101326}$ expressed as a decimal is MOST NEARLY 14.____
A. .0482 B. .00481 C. .0049 D. .00392

15. The reciprocal of the sum of 2/3 and 1/6 can be expressed as 15.____
A. 0.83 B. 1.20 C. 1.25 D. 1.50

16. Total land and building costs for a new commercial property equal $50 per square foot. 16.____
If the investors expect a 10 percent return on their costs, and if total operating expenses average 5 percent of total costs, annual gross rentals per square foot must be AT LEAST
A. $7.50 B. $8.50 C. $10.00 D. $12.00

17. The formula for computing the amount of annual deposit in a compound interest bearing account to provide a lump sum at the end of a period of years is 17.____
$X = \frac{r.L}{(1+r)^{n-1}}$ (X is the amount of annual deposit, r is the rate of interest, and n is the number of years and L = lump sum).
Using the formula, the annual amount of the deposit at the end of each year to accumulate $20,000 at the end of 3 years with interest at 2 percent on annual balances is
A. $6,120.00 B. $6,203.33 C. $6,535.09 D. $6,666.66

18. An investor sold two properties at $150,000 each. On one he made a 2.5 percent profit. On the other, he suffered a 25 percent loss. 18.____
The NET result of his sales was
A. neither a gain nor a loss
B. a $20,000 loss
C. a $75,000 gain
D. a $75,000 loss

19. A contractor decides to install a chain fence covering the perimeter of a parcel 75 feet wide and 112 feet in depth. 19.____
Which one of the following represents the number of feet to be covered?
A. 187
B. 364
C. 374
D. 8,400

20. A builder estimates he can build an average of 4½ one-family homes to an acre. There are 640 acres to one square mile. 20.____
Which one of the following CORRECTLY represents the number of one-family homes the builder would estimate he can build on one square mile?
A. 1,280
B. 1,920
C. 2,560
D. 2,880

21. $.01059 deposit at 7 percent interest will yield $1.00 in 30 years. 21.____
If a person deposited $1,059 at 7 percent interest on April 4, 1991, which one of the following amounts would represent the worth of this deposit on March 31, 2021?
A. $100
B. $1,000
C. $10,000
D. $100,000

22. A building has an economic life of forty years. 22.____
Assuming the building depreciates at a constant annual rate, which one of the following CORRECTLY represents the yearly percentage of depreciation?
A. 2.0%
B. 2.5%
C. 5.0%
D. 7.0%

23. A building produces a gross income of $200,000 with a net income of $20,000, before mortgage charges and capital recapture. The owner is able to increase the gross income 5 percent without a corresponding increase in operating costs. 23.____
The effect upon the net income will be an INCREASE of
A. 5%
B. 10%
C. 12.5%
D. 50%

24. The present value of $1.00 not payable for 8 years, and at 10 percent interest, is $.4665. 24.____
Which of the following amounts represents the PRESENT value of $1,000 payable 8 years hence at 10 percent interest?
A. $46.65
B. $466.50
C. $4,665.00
D. $46,650.00

25. The amount of real property taxes to be levied by a city is $100 million. The assessment roll subject to taxation shows an assessed valuation of $2 billion. 25.____
Which one of the following tax rates CORRECTLY represents the tax rate to be levied per $100 of assessed valuation?
A. $.50
B. $5.00
C. $50.00
D. $500.00

KEY (CORRECT ANSWERS)

1. A
2. C
3. A
4. C
5. A

6. B
7. D
8. C
9. B
10. C

11. C
12. C
13. B
14. B
15. B

16. A
17. C
18. B
19. C
20. D

21. D
22. B
23. D
24. B
25. B

SOLUTIONS TO PROBLEMS

1. \$597.45 + \$535.91 + \$639.91 + \$552.83 = \$2,326.11. Then, \$2,326.11 – (4)(\$525.50) = \$224.11

2. Death benefit = (\$13,486.50)($\frac{3}{7}$) ≈ \$5,779.92

3. $\frac{15}{28} \approx$ 53.57%

4. $\frac{11}{12} \approx$ 91.6% (closer to 91.7%)

5. $\frac{5}{12} \approx$ 41.7%

6. (\$4,725-\$3,213) ÷ \$4,725 = 32%

7. $\frac{28}{52} \approx$ 54%

8. $\frac{16}{52} \approx$ 30.7% (closer to 30.8%)

9. $\frac{2}{11} \approx$ 18.2%

10. (\$82,500 - \$70,500) ÷ \$70,500 = 17%

11. 17.5% = $\frac{175}{1000} = \frac{7}{40}$

12. 100% - 42% = 58% = $\frac{58}{100} = \frac{29}{50}$, closest to $\frac{7}{12}$ in selections

13. $\frac{\$10,000}{\$45,000} \approx$ 22.2%

14. 487/101,216 ≈ .00481

15. $\frac{2}{3} + \frac{1}{6} = \frac{5}{6}$ Then, $1 \div \frac{5}{6} = \frac{6}{5}$ = 1.20

16. (.15)(\$50) = \$7.50

17. x = (.02)(\$20,000)/[(1+.02)^3 – 1] = 400 ÷ .061208 ≈ \$6,535.09

18. Sold 150,000, 25% loss = paid 200,000, loss of \$50,000 Sold 150,000, 25% profit = paid 120,000, profit of 30,000 – 50,000 + 30,000 = 20,000 (loss)

19. Perimeter = (2)(75) + (2)(112) = 374 ft.

20. (640)(4½) = 2,880 homes

21. (1÷.01059)(1059) = \$100,000

22. 1÷4 = .025 = 2.5%

23. New gross income = (\$200,000)(X1.05) = \$210,000
Then, (\$210,000-\$200,000) ÷ \$20,000 = 50%

24. Let x = present value of \$1,000. Then, $\frac{\$1.00}{\$.4665} = \frac{\$1000}{x}$
Solving, x = \$466.50

25. Let x = tax rate. Then, $\frac{\$100{,}000{,}000}{\$2{,}000{,}000{,}000} = \frac{x}{\$100}$
Solving, x = \$5.00

TEST 3

DIRECTIONS: Each question or incomplete statement is followed by several suggested answers or completions. Select the one that BEST answers the question or completes the statement. *PRINT THE LETTER OF THE CORRECT ANSWER IN THE SPACE AT THE RIGHT.*

1. It is found that for the past three years the average weekly number of inspections per inspector ranged from 20 inspections to 40 inspections. 1.____
On the basis of this information, it is MOST reasonable to conclude that
   A. on the average, 30 inspections per week were made
   B. the average weekly number of inspections never fell below 20
   C. the performance of inspectors deteriorated over the three-year period
   D. the range in average weekly inspections was 60

Questions 2-4.

DIRECTIONS: Questions 2 through 4 are to be answered on the basis of the following information.

The number of students admitted to University X in 2019 from High School Y was 268 students. This represented 13.7 percent of University X's entering freshman classes. In 2020, it is expected that University X will admit 591 students from High School Y, which is expected to represent 19.4 percent of the 2020 entering freshman classes of University X.

2. Which of the following is CLOSEST estimate of the size of University's expected 2020 entering freshman classes? 2.____
_____ students
   A. 2,000 B. 2,500 C. 3,000 D. 3,500

3. Of the following, the expected percentage of increase from 2019 to 2020 in the number of students graduating from High School Y and entering University X as freshmen is MOST NEARLY 3.____
   A. 5.7% B. 20% C. 45% D. 120%

4. Assume that the cost of processing admission to University X from High School Y in 2019 was an average of $28. Also, that this was 1/3 more than the average cost of processing each of the other 2019 freshmen admissions to University X. 4.____
Then, the one of the following that MOST closely shows the total processing cost of all 2019 freshman admissions to University X is
   A. $6,500 B. $20,000 C. $30,000 D. $40,000

5. Assume that during the fiscal year 2019-2020, a bureau produced 20% more work units than it produced in the fiscal year 2018-2019. Also assume that during the fiscal year 2019-2020 that bureau's staff was 20% smaller than it was in the fiscal year 2018-2019. 5.____

On the basis of this information, it would be MOST proper to conclude that the number of work units produced per staff member in that bureau in the fiscal year 2019-2020 exceeded the number of work units produced per staff member in that bureau in the fiscal year 2018-2019 by which one of the following percentages?

A. 20% B. 25% C. 40% D. 50%

6. Assume that during the following fiscal years (FY), a bureau has received the following appropriations: 6.____

FY 2015-2016 - $200,000
FY 2016-2017 - $240,000
FY 2017-2018 - $280,000
FY 2018-2019 - $390,000
FY 2019-2020 - $505,000

The bureau's appropriation for which one of the following fiscal years showed the LARGEST percentage of increase over the bureau's appropriation for the immediately previous fiscal year?

A. FY 2016-2017
B. FY 2017-2018
C. FY 2018-2019
D. FY 2010-2020

7. Assume that the number of buses (U_t) required for a given line-haul system serving the Central Business District depends upon roundtrip time (t), capacity of bus (c), and the total number of people to be moved in a peak hour (P) in the major direction, i.e., in the morning and out in the evening. 7.____

The formula for the number of buses required is U_t =

A. Ptc B. $\frac{tP}{c}$ C. $\frac{cP}{t}$ D. $\frac{ct}{P}$

8. The area, in blocks, that can be served by a single stop for any maximum walking distance is given by the following formula: $a = 2w^2$. In this formula, a = the area served by a stop and w = maximum walking distance. 8.____

If people will tolerate a walk of up to three blocks, how many stops would be needed to service an area of 288 square blocks?

A. 9 B. 16 C. 18 D. 27

Questions 9-11.

DIRECTIONS: Questions 9 through 11 are to be answered on the basis of the following information.

In 2019, a police precinct records 456 cases of car thefts, which is 22.6 percent of all grand larcenies. In 2020, there were 560 such cases, which constituted 35% of the broader category.

9. The number of crimes in the broader category in 2020 was MOST NEARLY 9.____

A. 1,600 B. 1,700 C. 1,960 D. 2,800

10. The change from 2019 to 2020 in the number of crimes in the broader category represented MOST NEARLY a 10.____

A. 2.5% decrease
B. 10.1% increase
C. 12.5% increase
D. 20% decrease

11. In 2020, one out of every 6 of these crimes was solved. 11.____
This represents MOST NEARLY what percentage of the total number of crimes in the broader category that year?

A. 5.8
B. 6
C. 9.3
D. 12

12. Assume that a maintenance shop does 5 brake jobs to every 3 front-end jobs. It does 8,000 jobs altogether in a 240-day year. In one day, one worker can do 3 front-end jobs or 4 brake jobs. 12.____
About how many workers will be needed in the shop?

A. 3
B. 5
C. 10
D. 18

13. Assume that the price of a certain item declines by 6% one year, and then increases by 5 and 10 percent, respectively, during the next two years. 13.____
What is the OVERALL increase in price over the three-year period?

A. 4.2
B. 6
C. 8.6
D. 10.1

14. After finding the total percent change in a price (TO) over a three-year period, as in the preceding question, one could compute the average annual percent change in the price by using the formula 14.____

A. $(1+TC)^{1/3}$
B. $\frac{(1+TC)}{3}$
C. $(1+TC)^{1/3-1}$
D. $\frac{1}{(1+TC)^{1/3}-1}$

15. 357 is 6% of 15.____

A. 2,142
B. 5,950
C. 4,140
D. 5,900

16. In 2019, a department bought n pieces of a certain supply item for a total of \$x. In 2020, the department bought k percent fewer of the item but had to pay a total of g percent more for it. 16.____
Which of the following formulas is CORRECT for determining the average price per item in 2020?

A. $100\frac{xg}{nk}$
B. $\frac{x(100+g)}{n(100-k)}$
C. $\frac{x(100-g)}{n(100+k)}$
D. $\frac{x}{n} - 100\frac{g}{k}$

17. A sample of 18 income tax returns, each with 4 personal exemptions, is taken for 2019 and 2020. The breakdown is as follows in terms of income: 17.____

Average Gross Income (in thousands)	Number of Returns	
	2019	2020
40	6	2
80	10	11
120	2	5

There is a personal deduction per exemption of \$500.
There are no other expense deductions. In addition, there is an exclusion of \$3,000 for incomes less than \$50,000 and \$2,000 for incomes from \$50,000 to \$99,999.99. From \$100,000 upward there is no exclusion.

The average net taxable income for the samples in thousands for 2019 is MOST NEARLY
A. $67 B. $85 C. $10 D. $128

18. In the preceding question, the increase in average net taxable income for the sample (in thousands) between 2019 and 2020 is 18.____
A. 16 B. 20 C. 24 D. 34

19. Assume that supervisor S has four subordinates—A, B, C, and D. 19.____
The MAXIMUM number of relationships, assuming that all combinations are included, that can exist between S and his subordinates is
A. 28 B. 15 C. 7 D. 4

20. If the workmen's compensation insurance rate for clerical workers is 93 cents per $100 of wages, the total premium paid by a city whose clerical staff earns $8,765,000 is MOST NEARLY 20.____
A. $8,150 B. $81,515 C. $87,650 D. $93,765

21. Assume that a budget of $3,240,000,000 for the fiscal year beginning July 1, 2020 has been approved. A city sales tax is expected to provide $1,100,000,000; licenses, fees and sundry revenues ae expected to yield $121,600,000; the balance is to be raised from property taxes. A tax equalization board has appraised all property in the city at a fair value of $42,500,000,000. The council wishes to assess property at 60% of its fair value. 21.____
The tax rate would need to be MOST NEARLY _____ per $100 of assessed value.
A. $12.70 B. $10.65 C. $7.90 D. $4.00

22. Men's white linen handkerchiefs cost $12.90 for 3. 22.____
The cost per dozen handkerchiefs is
A. $77.40 B. $38.70 C. $144.80 D. $51.60

23. Assume that it is necessary to partition a room measuring 40 feet by 20 feet into eight smaller rooms of equal size. 23.____
Allowing no room for aisles, the MINIMUM amount of partitioning that would be needed is _____ feet.
A. 90 B. 100 C. 110 D. 140

24. Assume that two types of files have been ordered: 200 of type A and 100 of type B. When the files are delivered, the buyer discovers that 25% of each type is damaged. Of the remaining files, 20% of type A and 40% of type B are the wrong color. 24.____
The total number of files that are the WRONG COLOR is
A. 30 B. 40 C. 50 D. 60

25. In a unit of five inspectors, one inspector makes an average of 12 inspections a day, two inspectors make an average of 10 inspections a day, and two inspectors make an average of 9 inspections a day. 25.____
If in a certain week one of the inspectors who makes an average of nine inspections a day is out of work on Monday and Tuesday because of illness and all the inspectors do no inspections for half a day on Wednesday because of a special meeting, the number of inspections this unit can be expected to make in that week is MOST NEARLY
A. 215 B. 225 C. 230 D. 250

KEY (CORRECT ANSWERS)

1.	B	11.	A
2.	C	12.	C
3.	D	13.	C
4.	D	14.	C
5.	D	15.	B
6.	C	16.	B
7.	B	17.	A
8.	B	18.	A
9.	A	19.	B
10.	D	20.	B

21.	C
22.	D
23.	B
24.	D
25.	A

SOLUTIONS TO PROBLEMS

1. Since the number of weekly inspections ranged from 20 to 40, this implies that the average weekly number of inspections never fell below 20.

2. 591 ÷ 194 ≈ 3046, closest to 3,000 students

3. (591-268) ÷ 268 = 120%

4. Total processing cost = (268)(28) + (1,688)($21) = $42,952, closest to $40,000. [Note: Since 268 represents 13.7%, total freshman population = 268 ÷ .137 ≈ 1,956. Then, 1,956 – 268 = 1,688]

5. Let x = staff size in 2018-2019. Then, .80x = staff size in 2019-2020. Since the 2019-2020 staff produced 20% more work, this is represented by 1.20. However, to measure the productivity per staff member, the factor 1/.80 = 1.25 must also be used to equate the 2 staffs. Then, (1.20)(1.25) = 1.50. Thus, the 2019-2020 staff produced 50% more than the 2018-2019 staff.

6. The respective percent increases are ≈ 20%, 17%, 39%, 29%. The largest would be, over the previous fiscal year, for the current fiscal year 2018-2019

7. $\frac{P}{c}$ = number of buses needed per hour. If t = time (in hrs.), then U_t = tP.c

8. a = (2)(9) = 18 for 1 stop. Then, 288 ÷ 18 = 15 stops.

9. 560 ÷ .35 = 1600 grand larcenies.

10. 456 ÷ .226 = 2018; 560 ÷ .35 = 1600. Then, (1,600-2,018) ÷ 2,018 = -20% or a 20% decrease.

11. $(\frac{1}{6})(560) = 93\frac{1}{3}$. Then, $93\frac{1}{3}$ ÷ 1,600 = 5.8%

12. There are 5,000 brake jobs and 3,000 front-end jobs in one year.
5,000 ÷ 4 = 1,250 days, and 1,250 ÷ 240 ≈ 5.2. Also, 3,000 ÷ 3 = 1,000 days, and 1,000 ÷ 240 ≈ 4.2. Total number of workers needed ≈ 5.2 + 4.2 ≈ 10.

13. (.94)(1.05)(1.10) = 1.0857, which represents an overall increase by about 8.6%.

14. Average annual % change = $(1+TC)^{1/3} - 1 = (1.0857)^{1/3} - 1 \approx 2.8\%$.

15. 357 ÷ .06 = 5,950

16. In 2020, $(h)(1-\frac{k}{100})$ pieces cost $(x)(1 + \frac{g}{100})$ dollars. To calculate the cost for 1 piece (average cost), find the value of $[(x)(1 + \frac{G}{100})] \div [(n)(1 - \frac{K}{100})]$ = [(x)(100+g)/100].
[100/{n(100-k)}] = [x(100+g)]/[n(100-k)

17.

	#	Deductions Up to 50,000	
40,000	6	2000 3000	40,000-3,000-2,000 = 35,000 x 6
80,000	10	2000 2000	80,000-2,000-2,000 = 76,000 x 10
20,000	2	2000	= 118000 x 2

35,000 x 6 = 210,000 = 210
76,000 x 10 = 760,000 = 760
118,800 x 2 = 236,000 = 236
1206

1206 ÷ 18 = 67

18.

2020		Deductions			
40,000	2	2000	3000	35,000 x 2 =	70,000
80,000	11	2000	2000	76,000 x 11 =	836,000
120,000	5	2000		118,000 x 5 =	590,000
					1,496,000

1,496,000/18 = 83,111
83,111 – 67,000 = 16,111 = most nearly 16 (in thousands)

19. We are actually looking for the number of different groups of different sizes involving S. This reduces to $_4C_1 + {}_4C_2 + {}_4C_2 + {}_4C_4 = 4 + 6 + 4 + 1 = 15$. The notation $_nC_r$ means combinations of n things taken R at a time = [(n)(n-1)(n-2)(…)(n-R+1)]/[(R)(R-1)(…)(1)]. The 15 groups are: SA, SB, SC, SD, SAB, SAC, SAD, SBC, SBD, SCD, SABC, SABD, SACD, SBCD, SABCD.

20. Let x = total premiums. Then, $\frac{.93}{100} = \frac{X}{8,765,000}$ Solving, x = $81,515

21. The balance, raised from property taxes, = $3,240,000,000 - $1,100,000,000 – $121,600,000 = $2,018,400,000. Now, (.60)($42,500,000,000) = $25,500,000. The tax rate per $100 of assessed value = ($2,018,400,000)($100)(/$25,500,000,00 = $7.90.

22. A dozen costs ($12.90)($\frac{12}{3}$) = $51.60.

23. (40(20) ÷ 8 = 100 ft.

24. Total number of wrong-color files = (200)(.75)(.20)+(100)(.75)(.40) = 60

25. Weekly number of inspections = (12×5) + (10×5) + (10×5) + (9×5) + 9×5) = 250
Subtract: 9 Monday, 9 Tuesday, 25 Wednesday
Total: 250 – 9 – 9 – 25 = 207
Closest entry is choice A.

PHILOSOPHY, PRINCIPLES, PRACTICES, AND TECHNICS OF SUPERVISION, ADMINISTRATION, MANAGEMENT, AND ORGANIZATION

TABLE OF CONTENTS

PHILOSOPHY, PRINCIPLES, PRACTICES, AND TECHNICS
OF
SUPERVISION, ADMINISTRATION, MANAGEMENT, AND ORGANIZATION

MEANING OF SUPERVISION

The extension of the democratic philosophy has been accompanied by an extension in the scope of supervision. Modern leaders and supervisors no longer think of supervision in the narrow sense of being confined chiefly to visiting employees, supplying materials, or rating the staff. They regard supervision as being intimately related to all the concerned agencies of society, they speak of the supervisor's function in terms of "growth," rather than the "improvement" of employees.

This modern concept of supervision may be defined as follows: Supervision is leadership and the development of leadership within groups which are cooperatively engaged in inspection, research, training, guidance, and evaluation.

THE OLD AND THE NEW SUPERVISION

TRADITIONAL
1. Inspection
2. Focused on the employee
3. Visitation
4. Random and haphazard
5. Imposed and authoritarian
6. One person usually

MODERN
1. Study and analysis
2. Focused on aims, materials, methods, supervisors, employees, environment
3. Demonstrations, intervisitation, workshops, directed reading, bulletins, etc.
4. Definitely organized and planned (scientific)
5. Cooperative and democratic
6. Many persons involved (creative)

THE EIGHT (8) BASIC PRINCIPLES OF THE NEW SUPERVISION

I. Principle of Responsibility
Authority to act and responsibility for acting must be joined.
   A. If you give responsibility, give authority.
   B. Define employee duties clearly.
   C. Protect employees from criticism by others.
   D. Recognize the rights as well as obligations of employees.
   E. Achieve the aims of a democratic society insofar as it is possible within the area of your work.
   F. Establish a situation favorable to training and learning.
   G. Accept ultimate responsibility for everything done in your section, unit, office, division, department.
   H. Good administration and good supervision are inseparable.

II. Principle of Authority

The success of the supervisor is measured by the extent to which the power of authority is not used.

A. Exercise simplicity and informality in supervision
B. Use the simplest machinery of supervision
C. If it is good for the organization as a whole, it is probably justified.
D. Seldom be arbitrary or authoritative.
E. Do not base your work on the power of position or of personality.
F. Permit and encourage the free expression of opinions.

III. Principle of Self-Growth

The success of the supervisor is measured by the extent to which, and the speed with which, he is no longer needed.

A. Base criticism on principles, not on specifics.
B. Point out higher activities to employees.
C. Train for self-thinking by employees to meet new situations.
D. Stimulate initiative, self-reliance, and individual responsibility
E. Concentrate on stimulating the growth of employees rather than on removing defects.

IV. Principle of Individual Worth

Respect for the individual is a paramount consideration in supervision.

A. Be human and sympathetic in dealing with employees.
B. Don't nag about things to be done.
C. Recognize the individual differences among employees and seek opportunities to permit best expression of each personality.

V. Principle of Creative Leadership

The best supervision is that which is not apparent to the employee.

A. Stimulate, don't drive employees to creative action.
B. Emphasize doing good things.
C. Encourage employees to do what they do best.
D. Do not be too greatly concerned with details of subject or method.
E. Do not be concerned exclusively with immediate problems and activities.
F. Reveal higher activities and make them both desired and maximally possible.
G. Determine procedures in the light of each situation but see that these are derived from a sound basic philosophy.
H. Aid, inspire, and lead so as to liberate the creative spirit latent in all good employees.

VI. Principle of Success and Failure

There are no unsuccessful employees, only unsuccessful supervisors who have failed to give proper leadership.

A. Adapt suggestions to the capacities, attitudes, and prejudices of employees.
B. Be gradual, be progressive, be persistent.
C. Help the employee find the general principle; have the employee apply his own problem to the general principle.
D. Give adequate appreciation for good work and honest effort.
E. Anticipate employee difficulties and help to prevent them.
F. Encourage employees to do the desirable things they will do anyway.
G. Judge your supervision by the results it secures.

VII. Principle of Science

Successful supervision is scientific, objective, and experimental. It is based on facts, not on prejudices.

A. Be cumulative in results.
B. Never divorce your suggestions from the goals of training.
C. Don't be impatient of results.
D. Keep all matters on a professional, not a personal, level.
E. Do not be concerned exclusively with immediate problems and activities.
F. Use objective means of determining achievement and rating where possible.

VIII. Principle of Cooperation

Supervision is a cooperative enterprise between supervisor and employee.

A. Begin with conditions as they are.
B. Ask opinions of all involved when formulating policies.
C. Organization is as good as its weakest link.
D. Let employees help to determine policies and department programs.
E. Be approachable and accessible—physically and mentally.
F. Develop pleasant social relationships.

WHAT IS ADMINISTRATION

Administration is concerned with providing the environment, the material facilities, and the operational procedures that will promote the maximum growth and development of supervisors and employees. (Organization is an aspect and a concomitant of administration.)

There is no sharp line of demarcation between supervision and administration; these functions are intimately interrelated and, often, overlapping. They are complementary activities.

I. Practices Commonly Classed as "Supervisory"

A. Conducting employees' conferences
B. Visiting sections, units, offices, divisions, departments
C. Arranging for demonstrations
D. Examining plans
E. Suggesting professional reading
F. Interpreting bulletins
G. Recommending in-service training courses
H. Encouraging experimentation
I. Appraising employee morale
J. Providing for intervisitation

II. Practices Commonly Classified as "Administrative"

A. Management of the office
B. Arrangement of schedules for extra duties
C. Assignment of rooms or areas
D. Distribution of supplies
E. Keeping records and reports
F. Care of audio-visual materials
G. Keeping inventory records
H. Checking record cards and books

I. Programming special activities
J. Checking on the attendance and punctuality of employees

III. Practices Commonly Classified as Both "Supervisory" and "Administrative"
   A. Program construction
   B. Testing or evaluating outcomes
   C. Personnel accounting
   D. Ordering instructional materials

RESPONSIBILITIES OF THE SUPERVISOR

A person employed in a supervisory capacity must constantly be able to improve his own efficiency and ability. He represent the employer to the employees and only continuous self-examination can make him a capable supervisor.

Leadership and training are the supervisor's responsibility. An efficient working unit is one in which the employees work with the supervisor. It is his job to bring out the best in his employees. He must always be relaxed, courteous, and calm in his association with his employees. Their feelings are important, and a harsh attitude does not develop the most efficient employees.

COMPETENCES OF THE SUPERVISOR

I. Complete knowledge of the duties and responsibilities of his position.
II. To be able to organize a job, plan ahead, and carry through.
III. To have self-confidence and initiative.
IV. To be able to handle the unexpected situation and make quick decisions.
V. To be able to properly train subordinates in the positions they are best suited for.
VI. To be able to keep good human relations among his subordinates.
VII. To be able to keep good human relations between his subordinates and himself and to earn their respect and trust.

THE PROFESSIONAL SUPERVISOR-EMPLOYEE RELATIONSHIP

There are two kinds of efficiency: one kind is only apparent and is produced in organizations through the exercise of mere discipline; this is but a simulation of the second, or true, efficiency which springs from spontaneous cooperation. If you are a manager, no matter how great or small your responsibility, it is your job, in the final analysis, to create and develop this involuntary cooperation among the people whom you supervise. For, no matter how powerful a combination of money, machines, and materials a company may have, this is a dead and sterile thing without a team of willing, thinking, and articulate people to guide it.

The following 21 points are presented as indicative of the exemplary basic relationship that should exist between supervisor and employee:

1. Each person wants to be liked and respected by his fellow employee and wants to be treated with consideration and respect by his superior.
2. The most competent employee will make an error. However, in a unit where good relations exist between the supervisor and his employees, tenseness and fear do not exist. Thus, errors are not hidden or covered up, and the efficiency of a unit is not impaired.

3. Subordinates resent rules, regulations, or orders that are unreasonable or unexplained.
4. Subordinates are quick to resent unfairness, harshness, injustices, and favoritism.
5. An employee will accept responsibility if he knows that he will be complimented for a job well done, and not too harshly chastised for failure; that his supervisor will check the cause of the failure, and, if it was the supervisor's fault, he will assume the blame therefore. If it was the employee's fault, his supervisor will explain the correct method or means of handling the responsibility.
6. An employee wants to receive credit for a suggestion he has made, that is used. If a suggestion cannot be used, the employee is entitled to an explanation. The supervisor should not say "no" and close the subject.
7. Fear and worry slow up a worker's ability. Poor working environment can impair his physical and mental health. A good supervisor avoids forceful methods, threats, and arguments to get a job done.
8. A forceful supervisor is able to train his employees individually and as a team, and is able to motivate them in the proper channels.
9. A mature supervisor is able to properly evaluate his subordinates and to keep them happy and satisfied.
10. A sensitive supervisor will never patronize his subordinates.
11. A worthy supervisor will respect his employees' confidences.
12. Definite and clear-cut responsibilities should be assigned to each executive.
13. Responsibility should always be coupled with corresponding authority.
14. No change should be made in the scope or responsibilities of a position without a definite understanding to that effect on the part of all persons concerned.
15. No executive or employee, occupying a single position in the organization, should be subject to definite orders from more than one source.
16. Orders should never be given to subordinates over the head of a responsible executive. Rather than do this, the officer in question should be supplanted.
17. Criticisms of subordinates should, whoever possible, be made privately, and in no case should a subordinate be criticized in the presence of executives or employees of equal or lower rank.
18. No dispute or difference between executives or employees as to authority or responsibilities should be considered too trivial for prompt and careful adjudication.
19. Promotions, wage changes, and disciplinary action should always be approved by the executive immediately superior to the one directly responsible.
20. No executive or employee should ever be required, or expected, to be at the same time an assistant to, and critic of, another.
21. Any executive whose work is subject to regular inspection should, wherever practicable, be given the assistance and facilities necessary to enable him to maintain an independent check of the quality of his work.

MINI-TEXT IN SUPERVISION, ADMINISTRATION, MANAGEMENT, AND ORGANIZATION

I. Brief Highlights

Listed concisely and sequentially are major headings and important data in the field for quick recall and review.

A. Levels of Management

Any organization of some size has several levels of management. In terms of a ladder, the levels are:

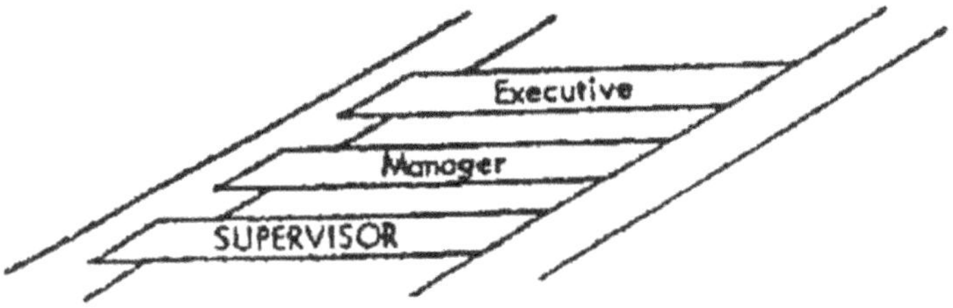

The first level is very important because it is the beginning point of management leadership.

B. What the Supervisor Must Learn

A supervisor must learn to:

1. Deal with people and their differences
2. Get the job done through people
3. Recognize the problems when they exist
4. Overcome obstacles to good performance
5. Evaluate the performance of people
6. Check his own performance in terms of accomplishment

C. A Definition of Supervisor

The term supervisor means any individual having authority, in the interests of the employer, to hire, transfer, suspend, lay-off, recall, promote, discharge, assign, reward, or discipline other employees or responsibility to direct them, or to adjust their grievances, or effectively to recommend such action, if, in connection with the foregoing, exercise of such authority is not of a merely routine or clerical nature but requires the use of independent judgment.

D. Elements of the Team Concept

What is involved in teamwork? The component parts are:

1. Members
2. A leader
3. Goals
4. Plans
5. Cooperation
6. Spirit

E. Principles of Organization

1. A team member must know what his job is.
2. Be sure that the nature and scope of a job are understood.
3. Authority and responsibility should be carefully spelled out.
4. A supervisor should be permitted to make the maximum number of decisions affecting his employees.
5. Employees should report to only one supervisor.
6. A supervisor should direct only as many employees as he can handle effectively.
7. An organization plan should be flexible.

8. Inspection and performance of work should be separate.
9. Organizational problems should receive immediate attention.
10. Assign work in line with ability and experience.

F. The Four Important Parts of Every Job
1. Inherent in every job is the *accountability* for results.
2. A second set of factors in every job is *responsibilities.*
3. Along with duties and responsibilities one must have the *authority* to act within certain limits without obtaining permission to proceed.
4. No job exists in a vacuum. The supervisor is surrounded by key *relationships.*

G. Principles of Delegation

Where work is delegated for the first time, the supervisor should think in terms of these questions:
1. Who is best qualified to do this?
2. Can an employee improve his abilities by doing this?
3. How long should an employee spend on this?
4. Are there any special problems for which he will need guidance?
5. How broad a delegation can I make?

H. Principles of Effective Communications
1. Determine the media.
2. To whom directed?
3. Identification and source authority.
4. Is communication understood?

I. Principles of Work Improvement
1. Most people usually do only the work which is assigned to them.
2. Workers are likely to fit assigned work into the time available to perform it.
3. A good workload usually stimulates output.
4. People usually do their best work when they know that results will be reviewed or inspected.
5. Employees usually feel that someone else is responsible for conditions of work, workplace layout, job methods, type of tools/equipment, and other such factors.
6. Employees are usually defensive about their job security.
7. Employees have natural resistance to change.
8. Employees can support or destroy a supervisor.
9. A supervisor usually earns the respect of his people through his personal example of diligence and efficiency.

J. Areas of Job Improvement

The areas of job improvement are quite numerous, but the most common ones which a supervisor can identify and utilize are:
1. Departmental layout
2. Flow of work
3. Workplace layout
4. Utilization of manpower
5. Work methods
6. Materials handling

7. Utilization
8. Motion economy

K. Seven Key Points in Making Improvements
1. Select the job to be improved
2. Study how it is being done now
3. Question the present method
4. Determine actions to be taken
5. Chart proposed method
6. Get approval and apply
7. Solicit worker participation

I. Corrective Techniques of Job Improvement

Specific Problems
1. Size of workload
2. Inability to meet schedules
3. Strain and fatigue
4. Improper use of men and skills
5. Waste, poor quality, unsafe conditions
6. Bottleneck conditions that hinder output
7. Poor utilization of equipment and machine
8. Efficiency and productivity of labor

General Improvement
1. Departmental layout
2. Flow of work
3. Work plan layout
4. Utilization of manpower
5. Work methods
6. Materials handling
7. Utilization of equipment
8. Motion economy

Corrective Techniques
1. Study with scale model
2. Flow chart study
3. Motion analysis
4. Comparison of units produced to standard allowance
5. Methods analysis
6. Flow chart and equipment study
7. Down time vs. running time
8. Motion analysis

M. A Planning Checklist
1. Objectives
2. Controls
3. Delegations
4. Communications
5. Resources
6. Manpower

7. Equipment
8. Supplies and materials
9. Utilization of time
10. Safety
11. Money
12. Work
13. Timing of improvements

N. Five Characteristics of Good Directions

In order to get results, directions must be:

1. Possible of accomplishment
2. Agreeable with worker interests
3. Related to mission
4. Planned and complete
5. Unmistakably clear

O. Types of Directions

1. Demands or direct orders
2. Requests
3. Suggestion or implication
4. volunteering

P. Controls

A typical listing of the overall areas in which the supervisor should establish controls might be:

1. Manpower
2. Materials
3. Quality of work
4. Quantity of work
5. Time
6. Space
7. Money
8. Methods

Q. Orienting the New Employee

1. Prepare for him
2. Welcome the new employee
3. Orientation for the job
4. Follow-up

R. Checklist for Orienting New Employees

	Yes	No
1. Do you appreciate the feelings of new employees when they first report for work?	___	___
2. Are you aware of the fact that the new employee must make a big adjustment to his job?	___	___
3. Have you given him good reasons for liking the job and the organization?	___	___
4. Have you prepared for his first day on the job?	___	___
5. Did you welcome him cordially and make him feel needed?	___	___

		Yes	No
6.	Did you establish rapport with him so that he feels free to talk and discuss matters with you?	___	___
7.	Did you explain his job to him and his relationship to you?	___	___
8.	Does he know that his work will be evaluated periodically on a basis that is fair and objective?	___	___
9.	Did you introduce him to his fellow workers in such a way that they are likely to accept him?	___	___
10.	Does he know what employee benefits he will receive?	___	___
11.	Does he understand the importance of being on the job and what to do if he must leave his duty station?	___	___
12.	Has he been impressed with the importance of accident prevention and safe practice?	___	___
13.	Does he generally know his way around the department?	___	___
14.	Is he under the guidance of a sponsor who will teach the right way of doing things?	___	___
15.	Do you plan to follow-up so that he will continue to adjust successfully to his job?	___	___

S. Principles of Learning
1. Motivation
2. Demonstration or explanation
3. Practice

T. Causes of Poor Performance
1. Improper training for job
2. Wrong tools
3. Inadequate directions
4. Lack of supervisory follow-up
5. Poor communications
6. Lack of standards of performance
7. Wrong work habits
8. Low morale
9. Other

U. Four Major Steps in On-The-Job Instruction
1. Prepare the worker
2. Present the operation
3. Tryout performance
4. Follow-up

V. Employees Want Five Things
1. Security
2. Opportunity
3. Recognition
4. Inclusion
5. Expression

W. Some Don'ts in Regard to Praise
1. Don't praise a person for something he hasn't done.
2. Don't praise a person unless you can be sincere.
3. Don't be sparing in praise just because your superior withholds it from you.
4. Don't let too much time elapse between good performance and recognition of it

X. How to Gain Your Workers' Confidence
Methods of developing confidence include such things as:
1. Knowing the interests, habits, hobbies of employees
2. Admitting your own inadequacies
3. Sharing and telling of confidence in others
4. Supporting people when they are in trouble
5. Delegating matters that can be well handled
6. Being frank and straightforward about problems and working conditions
7. Encouraging others to bring their problems to you
8. Taking action on problems which impede worker progress

Y. Sources of Employee Problems
On-the-job causes might be such things as:
1. A feeling that favoritism is exercised in assignments
2. Assignment of overtime
3. An undue amount of supervision
4. Changing methods or systems
5. Stealing of ideas or trade secrets
6. Lack of interest in job
7. Threat of reduction in force
8. Ignorance or lack of communications
9. Poor equipment
10. Lack of knowing how supervisor feels toward employee
11. Shift assignments

Off-the-job problems might have to do with:
1. Health
2. Finances
3. Housing
4. Family

Z. The Supervisor's Key to Discipline
There are several key points about discipline which the supervisor should keep in mind:
1. Job discipline is one of the disciplines of life and is directed by the supervisor.
2. It is more important to correct an employee fault than to fix blame for it.
3. Employee performance is affected by problems both on the job and off.
4. Sudden or abrupt changes in behavior can be indications of important employee problems.
5. Problems should be dealt with as soon as possible after they are identified.
6. The attitude of the supervisor may have more to do with solving problems than the techniques of problem solving.
7. Correction of employee behavior should be resorted to only after the supervisor is sure that training or counseling will not be helpful.

8. Be sure to document your disciplinary actions.
9. Make sure that you are disciplining on the basis of facts rather than personal feelings.
10. Take each disciplinary step in order, being careful not to make snap judgments, or decisions based on impatience.

AA. Five Important Processes of Management

1. Planning
2. Organizing
3. Scheduling
4. Controlling
5. Motivating

BB. When the Supervisor Fails to Plan

1. Supervisor creates impression of not knowing his job
2. May lead to excessive overtime
3. Job runs itself—supervisor lacks control
4. Deadlines and appointments missed
5. Parts of the work go undone
6. Work interrupted by emergencies
7. Sets a bad example
8. Uneven workload creates peaks and valleys
9. Too much time on minor details at expense of more important tasks

CC. Fourteen General Principles of Management

1. Division of work
2. Authority and responsibility
3. Discipline
4. Unity of command
5. Unity of direction
6. Subordination of individual interest to general interest
7. Remuneration of personnel
8. Centralization
9. Scalar chain
10. Order
11. Equity
12. Stability of tenure of personnel
13. Initiative
14. Esprit de corps

DD. Change

Bringing about change is perhaps attempted more often, and yet less well understood, than anything else the supervisor does. How do people generally react to change? (People tend to resist change that is imposed upon them by other individuals or circumstances.

Change is characteristic of every situation. It is a part of every real endeavor where the efforts of people are concerned.

1. Why do people resist change?
   People may resist change because of:
   a. Fear of the unknown
   b. Implied criticism
   c. Unpleasant experiences in the past
   d. Fear of loss of status
   e. Threat to the ego
   f. Fear of loss of economic stability

2. How can we best overcome the resistance to change?
   In initiating change, take these steps:
   a. Get ready to sell
   b. Identify sources of help
   c. Anticipate objections
   d. Sell benefits
   e. Listen in depth
   f. Follow up

II. Brief Topical Summaries

A. Who/What is the Supervisor?
1. The supervisor is often called the "highest level employee and the lowest level manager."
2. A supervisor is a member of both management and the work group. He acts as a bridge between the two.
3. Most problems in supervision are in the area of human relations, or people problems.
4. Employees expect: Respect, opportunity to learn and to advance, and a sense of belonging, and so forth.
5. Supervisors are responsible for directing people and organizing work. Planning is of paramount importance.
6. A position description is a set of duties and responsibilities inherent to a given position.
7. It is important to keep the position description up-to-date and to provide each employee with his own copy.

B. The Sociology of Work
1. People are alike in many ways; however, each individual is unique.
2. The supervisor is challenged in getting to know employee differences. Acquiring skills in evaluating individuals is an asset.
3. Maintaining meaningful working relationships in the organization is of great importance.
4. The supervisor has an obligation to help individuals to develop to their fullest potential.
5. Job rotation on a planned basis helps to build versatility and to maintain interest and enthusiasm in work groups.
6. Cross training (job rotation) provides backup skills.

7. The supervisor can help reduce tension by maintaining a sense of humor, providing guidance to employees, and by making reasonable and timely decisions. Employees respond favorably to working under reasonably predictable circumstances.
8. Change is characteristic of all managerial behavior. The supervisor must adjust to changes in procedures, new methods, technological changes, and to a number of new and sometimes challenging situations.
9. To overcome the natural tendency for people to resist change, the supervisor should become more skillful in initiating change.

C. Principles and Practices of Supervision

1. Employees should be required to answer to only one superior.
2. A supervisor can effectively direct only a limited number of employees, depending upon the complexity, variety, and proximity of the jobs involved.
3. The organizational chart presents the organization in graphic form. It reflects lines of authority and responsibility as well as interrelationships of units within the organization.
4. Distribution of work can be improved through an analysis using the "Work Distribution Chart."
5. The "Work Distribution Chart" reflects the division of work within a unit in understandable form.
6. When related tasks are given to an employee, he has a better chance of increasing his skills through training.
7. The individual who is given the responsibility for tasks must also be given the appropriate authority to insure adequate results.
8. The supervisor should delegate repetitive, routine work. Preparation of recurring reports, maintaining leave and attendance records are some examples.
9. Good discipline is essential to good task performance. Discipline is reflected in the actions of employees on the job in the absence of supervision.
10. Disciplinary action may have to be taken when the positive aspects of discipline have failed. Reprimand, warning, and suspension are examples of disciplinary action.
11. If a situation calls for a reprimand, be sure it is deserved and remember it is to be done in private.

D. Dynamic Leadership

1. A style is a personal method or manner of exerting influence.
2. Authoritarian leaders often see themselves as the source of power and authority.
3. The democratic leader often perceives the group as the source of authority and power.
4. Supervisors tend to do better when using the pattern of leadership that is most natural for them.
5. Social scientists suggest that the effective supervisor use the leadership style that best fits the problem or circumstances involved.
6. All four styles—telling, selling, consulting, joining—have their place. Using one does not preclude using the other at another time.

7. The theory X point of view assumes that the average person dislikes work, will avoid it whenever possible, and must be coerced to achieve organizational objectives.
8. The theory Y point of view assumes that the average person considers work to be a natural as play, and, when the individual is committed, he requires little supervision or direction to accomplish desired objectives.
9. The leader's basic assumptions concerning human behavior and human nature affect his actions, decisions, and other managerial practices.
10. Dissatisfaction among employees is often present, but difficult to isolate. The supervisor should seek to weaken dissatisfaction by keeping promises, being sincere and considerate, keeping employees informed, and so forth.
11. Constructive suggestions should be encouraged during the natural progress of the work.

E. Processes for Solving Problems
1. People find their daily tasks more meaningful and satisfying when they can improve them.
2. The causes of problems, or the key factors, are often hidden in the background. Ability to solve problems often involves the ability to isolate them from their backgrounds. There is some substance to the cliché that some persons "can't see the forest for the trees."
3. New procedures are often developed from old ones. Problems should be broken down into manageable parts. New ideas can be adapted from old one.
4. People think differently in problem-solving situations. Using a logical, patterned approach is often useful. One approach found to be useful includes these steps:
    a. Define the problem
    b. Establish objectives
    c. Get the facts
    d. Weigh and decide
    e. Take action
    f. Evaluate action

F. Training for Results
1. Participants respond best when they feel training is important to them.
2. The supervisor has responsibility for the training and development of those who report to him.
3. When training is delegated to others, great care must be exercised to insure the trainer has knowledge, aptitude, and interest for his work as a trainer.
4. Training (learning) of some type goes on continually. The most successful supervisor makes certain the learning contributes in a productive manner to operational goals.
5. New employees are particularly susceptible to training. Older employees facing new job situations require specific training, as well as having need for development and growth opportunities.
6. Training needs require continuous monitoring.
7. The training officer of an agency is a professional with a responsibility to assist supervisors in solving training problems.

8. Many of the self-development steps important to the supervisor's own growth are equally important to the development of peers and subordinates. Knowledge of these is important when the supervisor consults with others on development and growth opportunities.

G. Health, Safety, and Accident Prevention
1. Management-minded supervisors take appropriate measures to assist employees in maintaining health and in assuring safe practices in the work environment.
2. Effective safety training and practices help to avoid injury and accidents.
3. Safety should be a management goal. All infractions of safety which are observed should be corrected without exception.
4. Employees' safety attitude, training and instruction, provision of safe tools and equipment, supervision, and leadership are considered highly important factors which contribute to safety and which can be influenced directly by supervisors.
5. When accidents do occur, they should be investigated promptly for very important reasons, including the fact that information which is gained can be used to prevent accidents in the future.

H. Equal Employment Opportunity
1. The supervisor should endeavor to treat all employees fairly, without regard to religion, race, sex, or national origin.
2. Groups tend to reflect the attitude of the leader. Prejudice can be detected even in very subtle form. Supervisors must strive to create a feeling of mutual respect and confidence in every employee.
3. Complete utilization of all human resources is a national goal. Equitable consideration should be accorded women in the work force, minority-group members, the physically and mentally handicapped, and the older employee. The important question is: "Who can do the job?"
4. Training opportunities, recognition for performance, overtime assignments, promotional opportunities, and all other personnel actions are to be handled on an equitable basis.

I. Improving Communications
1. Communications is achieving understanding between the sender and the receiver of a message. It also means sharing information—the creation of understanding.
2. Communication is basic to all human activity. Words are means of conveying meanings; however, real meanings are in people.
3. There are very practical differences in the effectiveness of one-way, impersonal, and two-way communications. Words spoken face-to-face are better understood. Telephone conversations are effective, but lack the rapport of person-to-person exchanges. The whole person communicates.
4. Cooperation and communication in an organization go hand in hand. When there is a mutual respect between people, spelling out rules and procedures for communicating is unnecessary.
5. There are several barriers to effective communications. These include failure to listen with respect and understanding, lack of skill in feedback, and misinterpreting the meanings of words used by the speaker. It is also common

practice to listen to what we want to hear, and tune out things we do not want to hear.

6. Communication is management's chief problem. The supervisor should accept the challenge to communicate more effectively and to improve interagency and intra-agency communications.
7. The supervisor may often plan for and conduct meetings. The planning phase is critical and may determine the success or the failure of a meeting.
8. Speaking before groups usually requires extra effort. Stage fright may never disappear completely, but it can be controlled.

J. Self-Development

1. Every employee is responsible for his own self-development.
2. Toastmaster and toastmistress clubs offer opportunities to improve skills in oral communications.
3. Planning for one's own self-development is of vital importance. Supervisors know their own strengths and limitations better than anyone else.
4. Many opportunities are open to aid the supervisor in his developmental efforts, including job assignments; training opportunities, both governmental and non-governmental—to include universities and professional conferences and seminars.
5. Programmed instruction offers a means of studying at one's own rate.
6. Where difficulties may arise from a supervisor's being away from his work for training, he may participate in televised home study or correspondence courses to meet his self-development needs.

K. Teaching and Training

1. The Teaching Process
   Teaching is encouraging and guiding the learning activities of students toward established goals. In most cases this process consists of five steps: preparation, presentation, summarization, evaluation, and application.

   a. Preparation
      Preparation is two-fold in nature; that of the supervisor and the employee. Preparation by the supervisor is absolutely essential to success. He must know what, when, where, how, and whom he will teach. Some of the factors that should be considered are:
      1) The objectives
      2) The materials needed
      3) The methods to be used
      4) Employee participation
      5) Employee interest
      6) Training aids
      7) Evaluation
      8) Summarization

      Employee preparation consists in preparing the employee to receive the material. Probably the most important single factor in the preparation of the employee is arousing and maintaining his interest. He must know the objectives of the training, why he is there, how the material can be used, and its importance to him.

b. Presentation
In presentation, have a carefully designed plan and follow it. The plan should be accurate and complete, yet flexible enough to meet situations as they arise. The method of presentation will be determined by the particular situation and objectives.

c. Summary
A summary should be made at the end of every training unit and program. In addition, there may be internal summaries depending on the nature of the material being taught. The important thing is that the trainee must always be able to understand how each part of the new material relates to the whole.

d. Application
The supervisor must arrange work so the employee will be given a chance to apply new knowledge or skills while the material is still clear in his mind and interest is high. The trainee does not really know whether he has learned the material until he has been given a chance to apply it. If the material is not applied, it loses most of its value.

e. Evaluation
The purpose of all training is to promote learning. To determine whether the training has been a success or failure, the supervisor must evaluate this learning.
In the broadest sense, evaluation includes all the devices, methods, skills, and techniques used by the supervisor to keep himself and the employees informed as to their progress toward the objectives they are pursuing. The extent to which the employee has mastered the knowledge, skills, and abilities, or changed his attitudes, as determined by the program objectives, is the extent to which instruction has succeeded or failed.
Evaluation should not be confined to the end of the lesson, day, or program but should be used continuously. We shall note later the way this relates to the rest of the teaching process.

2. Teaching Methods
A teaching method is a pattern of identifiable student and instructor activity used in presenting training material.
All supervisors are faced with the problem of deciding which method should be used at a given time.

a. Lecture
The lecture is direct oral presentation of material by the supervisor. The present trend is to place less emphasis on the trainer's activity and more on that of the trainee.

b. Discussion
Teaching by discussion or conference involves using questions and other techniques to arouse interest and focus attention upon certain areas, and by doing so creating a learning situation. This can be one of the most

valuable methods because it gives the employees an opportunity to express their ideas and pool their knowledge.

c. Demonstration
The demonstration is used to teach how something works or how to do something. It can be used to show a principle or what the results of a series of actions will be. A well-staged demonstration is particularly effective because it shows proper methods of performance in a realistic manner.

d. Performance
Performance is one of the most fundamental of all learning techniques or teaching methods. The trainee may be able to tell how a specific operation should be performed but he cannot be sure he knows how to perform the operation until he has done so.
As with all methods, there are certain advantages and disadvantages to each method.

e. Which Method to Use
Moreover, there are other methods and techniques of teaching. It is difficult to use any method without other methods entering into it. In any learning situation, a combination of methods is usually more effective than any one method alone.

Finally, evaluation must be integrated into the other aspects of the teaching-learning process.

It must be used in the motivation of the trainees; it must be used to assist in developing understanding during the training; and it must be related to employee application of the results of training.

This is distinctly the role of the supervisor.

www.ingramcontent.com/pod-product-compliance
Lightning Source LLC
Chambersburg PA
CBHW081816300426
44116CB00014B/2387
* 9 7 8 1 7 9 9 3 1 6 8 1 7 *